www.advertising

RICHARD ADAMS

SERIES CONSULTANT
ALASTAIR CAMPBELL

WATSON-GUPTILL
PUBLICATIONS
New York

The information
contained in this book is
given without warranty
and, while every
precaution has been
taken in compiling the
book, neither the author
nor the publisher
assumes any
responsibility or liability
whatsoever to any
person or entity with
respect to any errors
which may exist in the
book, nor for any loss of
data which may occur as
the result of such errors
or for the efficacy or
performance of any
product or process
described in the book.

This book was conceived,
designed and produced
by The Ilex Press Ltd
Cambridge
England

Sales Office
The Old Candlemakers
West Street, Lewes
East Sussex
BN7 2NZ

Creative Director:
Alastair Campbell
Executive Publisher:
Sophie Collins
Art Director:
Peter Bridgewater
Editorial Director:
Steve Luck
Design Manager:
Tony Seddon
Project Editor:
Chris Middleton
Designers:
Jane and Chris Lanaway

www.designdirectories.com

Library of Congress
Cataloging-in-Publication
Number 2002117050

ISBN 0-8230-5861-1

Originated and printed
by Hong Kong Graphics
and Printing Ltd, China

All websites mentioned
in this book were current
at the time of writing, but
due to the changing
nature of the Internet, it
is possible that some are
now hosting different
content. The author and
publisher cannot accept
liability for these changes
and apologize for any
inconvenience.

INTRODUCTION

Society occasionally witnesses a seismic shift in communications. The introduction of newspapers, the telegraph, telephony, radio, and television have all transformed the way people interact with each other, and have created new business opportunities and business models. The World Wide Web is the basis of another shift in the way people interact, wherever they are in the world.

The protocols behind the Web allow text, images, sound, video, animations, and games to be accessed via a browser from anywhere in the world where there is a phone line. The Web has truly burst into life, and it is a life that is increasingly rich in color, movement, and innovation.

Endless potential

As a medium, the early Web was slow, limited, and text-based, but its potential was obvious from day one. Businesses soon saw that basing business processes—perhaps even the entire enterprise—on the Web could be a fast and efficient way of not just interacting with customers, but establishing a one-to-one dialog.

The rush to stake a claim on this virgin territory, and the inevitable rash of "me too" enterprises, saw billions of dollars being poured into new Internet ventures ("dot coms"). In order for any one of these thousands of new businesses to be seen and heard, untold amounts of money were poured into marketing, as well as building the infrastructures to support so many new ventures. Companies rapidly became vastly overvalued compared with their revenues and profitability (few, if any, turned a profit fast enough to survive their levels of expenditure). A dot-com crash swiftly followed the dot-com boom.

The Web, however, did not go away. In fact—to the surprise of many pundits—it has started taking the place of "traditional" media as a means of accessing news fast, and of creating communities built around shared interests, passions, and business opportunities.

Businesses using the Web do so now as part of a rational business process, not just as "the thing to do" because they are concerned about being left behind by their competitors in a technological arms race. It's now a low-cost channel for doing business directly with customers: and that means potentially valuable one-on-one advertising opportunities.

Other media are changing as a result. Television has harnessed the Internet to become interactive, and mobile phones have mutated into devices that can be used for both voice and data calls. The next generation of devices promises richer video and audio environments on the move, although neither the technology nor the demand for services have yet been proved.

TV itself can now offer "on demand" commerce via a set-top box, and can be used to view the Web and send email. Recent games consoles also offer a route onto the Internet, as well as the ability to play other types of media.

1

2

1 | 2
Digital media, and the Web in particular, have seen a plethora of different ad formats. These range from games to SMS (short messaging service) based ads.

3
Websites that sell advertising space have also spent a lot of time designing their content to allow for the best placement of advertising material.

4
As in the case of *The Japan Times* online, the content can be arranged to provide maximum visibility for ads.

It is clear that we are only at the beginning of a long process of convergence. The media we use are rapidly evolving, which means that business models and the ways in which businesses can address their customers will also evolve. All of this is exciting for advertisers.

Individuals can already be targeted specifically so that each user receives only their requested content. This is a profound shift from a "one-to-many" distribution model to a "one-to-one" opportunity.

This book will examine the role of advertising in the digital space. It will look at prime examples of the medium from around the world and will also show the ways in which digital advertising is creating innovative, low-cost, and highly targeted opportunities, while expanding into other media related to the Web.

7

8

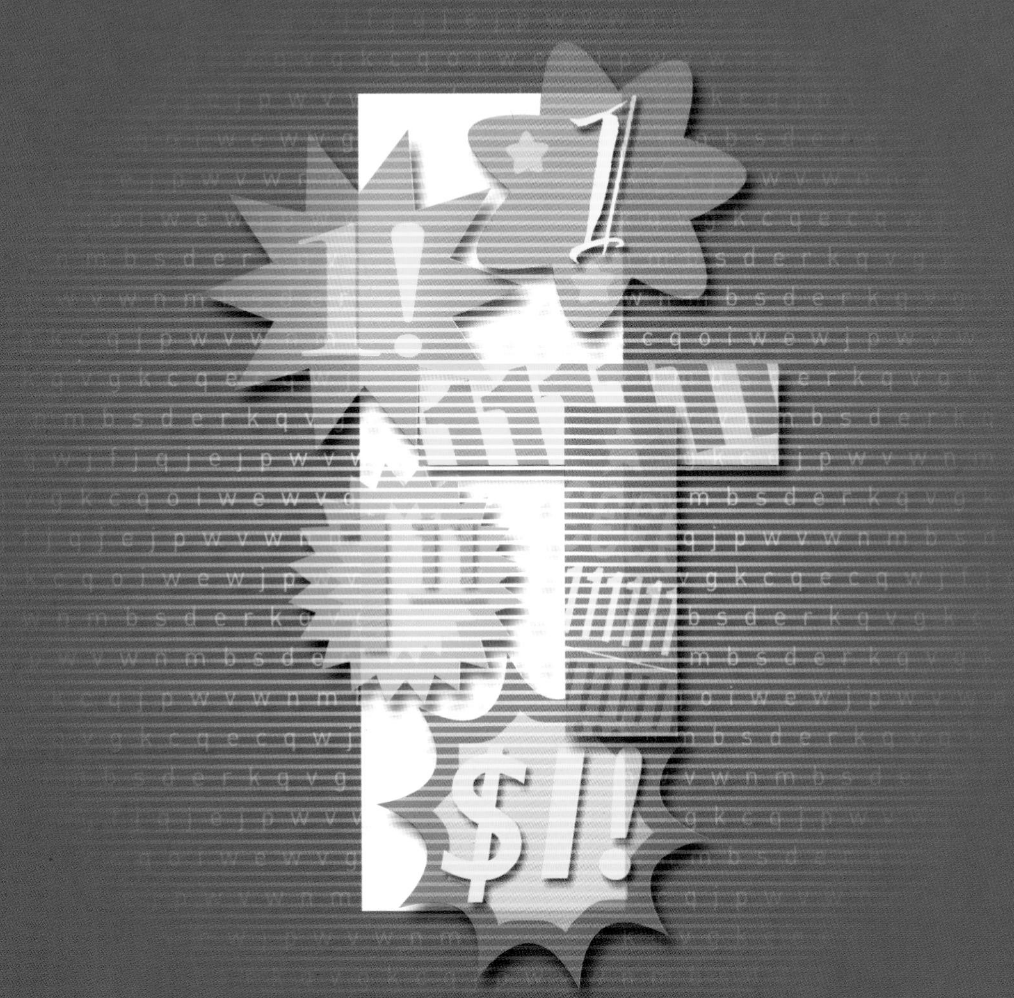

VIRTUAL HOARDINGS

The explosive growth of the Web has seen large amounts of content and commerce being transferred to and delivered via the Web. Traditional brands have moved into the space, corporate sites abound, and a variety of new companies have appeared specifically as online businesses (some of them spin-offs from major corporations). Users can download video and audio, watch and interact with animations, gain access to a whole world of music and audio, read online magazines, and access TV and radio content. Users can also make and join communities and communicate with users around the world, at any time.

As with any major medium, one of the ways of financially supporting this growth and its ever-mutating variety of services has been to accept advertising. Newspapers, TV, and radio channels long ago built advertising revenue into their business models—indeed, most magazines exist to sell advertising to a clearly defined user base.

In accepting adverts, newspapers have been able to keep down their cover prices and attract readers, who in turn attract more advertisers. This is an economic virtual circle that, provided it is balanced, can ensure the long-term health of a newspaper. Television advertisements have long been accepted as a way of providing funding for programming.

10

2

ENGLISH   ENGLISH (USA)   DEUTSCH   FRANCAIS   ESPAÑOL
ITALIANO   PORTUGUÊS   PORTUGUÊS (BR)   日本語   한국어

NIKEFOOTBALL.COM

LANGUE   SCEGLI LA LINGUA   ELIGE TU IDIOMA   ESCOLHE O TEU IDIOMA   ES

NIKEFOOTBALL.COM

LOADING 37 kb

1

3

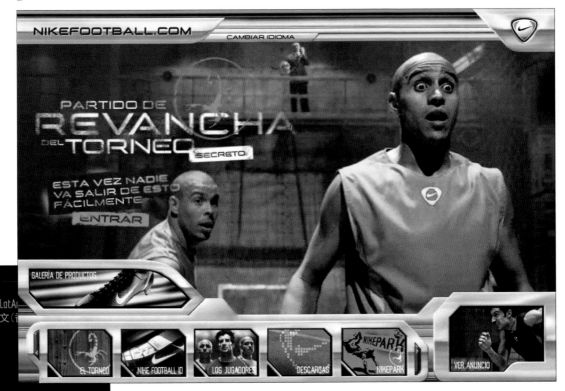

NIKEFOOTBALL.COM

CAMBIAR IDIOMA

PARTIDO DE
REVANCHA
DEL TORNEO SECRETO

ESTA VEZ NADIE
VA SALIR DE ESTO
FÁCILMENTE

ENTRAR

GALERÍA DE PRODUCTOS

EL TORNEO · NIKE FOOTBALL ID · LOS JUGADORES · DESCARGAS · NIKEPARK · VER ANUNCIO

1 | 2 | 3
Nike's site for the FIFA soccer world cup in 2002 was typical of the high-gloss rich media ad formats that have appeared in recent years.

Advertising power

Notwithstanding the arguments that the balance on television may have tilted too far in the direction of commerce (to the point where content cannot be made without advertiser input or indeed interference), it is nonetheless a multibillion-dollar industry. Products, companies and individuals' careers can be made or broken by successful or failing advertising.

The rise of digital media has also seen a plethora of websites whose business models revolve around selling advertising opportunities. To facilitate this, a range of formats and standards has been arrived at, which largely evolved from the demands of the early big traffic sites.

Among these were banner adverts, a format where the ad is a long thin strip of information that can be easily inserted on a site so that users see them as they download the pages. Banners are also limited in memory size. They have to be small so that they download swiftly and do not interfere with the smooth operation of the host website

Advertisers jumped at banner ads when they first appeared as a way of reaching this new, potentially worldwide audience in a personalized, meaningful way. Sites saw a mushrooming growth in online advertising as agencies and clients alike increased their budgets and spent money indiscriminately. The future looked rosy as advertisers envisaged a move from complex, expensive, multinational campaigns to ones that could be targeted at the individual wherever they were. The future had never looked so good...

JUST HOW RELEVANT IS ADVERTISING ON THE WEB?

As advertisers dreamed of attaining perfect penetration through individually targeted digital ads, the future certainly did look rosy—for a while. The huge surge of optimism about the "new economy" of the Internet—sustainable high growth and low inflation—quickly evaporated as real-world economics returned.

Until the dot-com crash, ad spend increased as the hype surrounding the Web grew into a frenzy. Agencies created entire new divisions to deal with the perceived flood of new advertising opportunities and dollars. The only cloud on the horizon for advertisers was their concern about the banner format and how effective it actually was. The more serious cloud, of course, was the billions of dollars being poured into marketing unsustainable businesses, as venture capital was burned through in months by ventures who needed years to build revenues and profits.

On the face of it, the banner ad had—and still has—its attractions. When a user clicks on a banner, that click can be recorded so that a business can accurately track their campaigns in terms of how many people actually read the ad and go through to the site.

This so-called Click-through rate (CTR) (*see page 14*) became the foundation of many a business model. In the very early days, the concept worked very successfully and CTRs were high, but as banners proliferated, questions arose about their efficacy. There were even studies undertaken into "banner blindness." CTRs began to be recorded at 0.1% and even lower. As the recession at the turn of the millennium hit, businesses began to question whether it was worth the money to advertise on the Web when, for example, a TV campaign could get a very large response and offer more cost effectiveness.

1 | 2 | 3 | 4
From professional boxing to footwear and from furniture, through airlines to cookery, businesses see the Web as a good way of getting instant access to customers. As can be seen in these images, even within the standard banner format, effective advertising can be created for any audience.

12

3

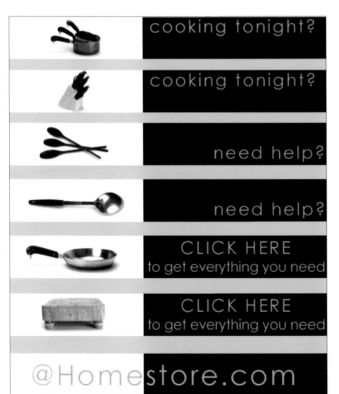

4

Despite the setbacks to the economic model, digital advertising has not gone away. In fact, it has diversified and grown into an industry that has at last replaced naïve optimism with hard-headed business planning. More important, businesses have begun to appreciate the unique services that the Internet offers.

In recent years the Web has become one element of overall corporate marketing and advertising strategies. In fact, it is often the way in which a cross-media campaign can be linked, managed, and perpetuated.

The Web and the business it supports have grown up together. CTR is no longer the only measure of success. Impact and awareness are now tracked and newer forms of ads have arrived that provide value-for-money content. This means that the banner ad is now just one of many possible advertising solutions, many of them innovative, eye-catching, self-perpetuating, and unique to the Internet environment.

The fact is that digital media in general, and the Web in particular, offer advertisers unique ways to reach different audiences. Using the Web, a company can produce incredibly effective campaigns that can reach target audiences that go beyond standard demographic groupings. Using the information gathered from one campaign, companies can identify new customers—and new groups of customers—as they emerge.

Where the Web is particularly effective in advertising terms, is in reaching communities that share an interest. Instead of relying on age, income, and location, as advertisers used to do, companies can target their products at people who have demonstrated an interest (or a potential interest) in the product, rather than by making assumptions based on demographic information.

This represents a fundamental shift in the way that advertisers are interacting with consumers—one that is now reflected in the types of campaigns and media used in contemporary digital advertising.

13

THE BUSINESS OF ONLINE ADVERTISING

The business of online advertising has grown enormously despite the economic problems of recent years. Digital agencies have grown and merged, broken away, and been merged again into larger agencies. What has emerged is a robust multibillion-dollar industry that has its own practices and rules.

Some of the common terminology is described below. It is by no means an exhaustive list, but it does cover most of the basic concepts of online advertising. These terms are often used, but equally often misunderstood.

Page view is simply the viewing of a page by a user.

Click through/ad click is the action of clicking on an advertisement by a user.

Cost per click is a concept much used by media agencies and refers to the cost for every person that actually clicks on an advertisement. This is usually charged by the thousand and does rely on users being active in order to pay.

Click-through rate is usually measured as the percentage of users that click on an advertisement. This is often what results of campaigns are based on.

CPM (cost per 1,000) is the rate that reflects the cost per thousand ad views for a particular site as charged by the content site to the media agency.

Cost per action is the amount paid when a user clicks on an advertisement, goes through to a site, then actually performs an action, such as responding to a request for information.

These concepts form the basis of pricing in online advertising. It is often difficult to work out which method is most cost effective. Cost per click and click-through rates offer such an easy way of measuring performance that advertisers are immediately attracted to them. They can use the figures to work out whether the campaign is successful and base their further business decisions on them. However, the figures are by no means perfect as ways of measuring performance.

The business of online advertising is a complex one, and is not made any easier by the rapid evolution of formats. The complex nature of any operation that involves placing ads across so many potential sites, while still keeping an eye on CTRs, means that many third-party companies have appeared who offer nothing but these specific skills.

Digital ads are now usually served by third-party companies that buy space on sites, and subsequently use further companies to serve different ads to different sites as and when requested. These companies are investing millions of dollars in research, analysis, and tracking tools and it is these companies that supply agencies with the forecasts and the results necessary to ensure ongoing success.

1 | 2 | 3 | 4

Search for ad services on a search engine and many results appear. Ad serving and management is certainly big business. Companies such as the ones here offer good advice to advertisers and agencies alike. In some cases, agencies have formed strategic partnerships with ad-management companies to make the process easier. Looking through their sites, it is usually possible to find the answers to most of the questions that crop up at the planning stage.

FROM BILLBOARD TO BANNER

In newspapers, advertisers can buy a range of formats. They can advertise using solely text in classified sections. They can buy sections of pages or even whole pages for high-impact, visual campaigns. Sometimes they can even print supplements that are inserted into the magazines and newspapers and are reminiscent in style of actual newspaper content. On television, advertisers can sponsor events and specific programmes, or create ads that are shown in designated ad breaks. Radio works in a similar way.

All of these formats rely directly on a range of metrics to measure their effectiveness. It is relatively simple to ask someone who calls an advertised phone number where they saw the number. Likewise, it is clear that if an ad is placed in a top-rated programme slot over the life of the campaign and sales rise, then it is likely that the ad campaign is responsible.

Billboards too have been used with great effectiveness, but as with TV, unless they have a "call to action" it is difficult to place a figure against success or failure.

16

1

2

3

4

5

1 | 2 | 3 | 4
These AT&T
skyscraper-format
banners clearly show
how digital ads tend
to be based on calls
to action. The user is
taken through an
animation after which
they are invited to
click to learn more.

5 | 6 | 7 | 8 | 9
This unique online
benefit can also be
seen in these banners
for the UK's
Automobile
Association (AA)
where after playing a
simple game, the user
is invited to "click
thru."

The move to digital media has been largely sold on the promise of accurate measurement and data. Clearly it hasn't always been the case. As we discussed earlier, banner ads have dwindled in popularity and reach. So why are they still there? Among the reasons for this is the fact that the placement of banner ads has become crucial. Gone are the days when they were placed indiscriminately on large sites. Now agencies can decide on which webpage they appear, and which groups of users can see them. This is part of the dialog between businesses and consumers that only the Web can create and promote.

17

The humble banner

"Smart ads" are now used within search engines. They are served when certain key words are entered into the search box. When the search results appear onscreen, a relevant ad also appears. If, for example, someone searches for "football", adverts related to football crop up when the search is complete. This ensures a high-impact, low-waste presence for advertisers looking only to target genuine potential customers. After all, the Web is a "pull" medium, not a "push" or broadcast one, so it is natural that advertising should chase the benefits of the Web by only appearing to surfers who are looking to pull specific types of information off the Internet.

Banners can still be central to this process, because when it is known what an individual user is looking for, then a banner can do two things. It can act to raise awareness of an issue or product related to the content onscreen, and it can act as a signpost that can take the user directly to the relevant website. It is this evolution of usage that has kept the banner alive.

The key to most digital advertising is that it can have a call to action within it that takes a user directly to the "store." Unlike TV, radio, and billboard, one click can take the user straight into a commercial environment where money can change hands.

BANNER FORMATS

The Internet has forced advertisers and their agencies to rethink the way they market their wares. On the one hand, it offers powerful new opportunities to reach customers; on the other, it imposes technical limitations on designers used to old media.

Designing a sizeable website often involves a fight to get as many key elements as possible above the "fold" of the page—the point where, depending on your screen size, you need to start scrolling down to see more. Space in the top half of a webpage is like gold dust—especially if it's within a click of the home page.

The exact dimensions of this golden real estate depend on a site's target screen size, which will, in turn, depend on its target audience, but let's take 590 x 225 pixels as a likely average. Vying to get in here will be a logo, a strapline, a line or so of navigation, a page title or headline and, of course, an advert or two. The outcome is that everything ends up small, with particular limitations imposed on the height.

The solution?

The humble banner

A measly 468 x 60 pixel eyesore, more than four times wider than it is high, the banner ad is rarely big enough to show a pair of eyes, let alone a model's face or a complete product shot. The banner ad has less pixels than a printed poster has square centimetres.

Of course, you don't have to use the whole space if you require a different shape for your ad; the dimensions are simply an agreed conventional maximum. But marketing people are loathe to "waste" their space when they could sell all of it to another client at the full rate.

Banner ads' dimensions aren't the only headache for designers who are more used to working in inches and print. The file size challenge is enough to give them nightmares. A digital image for a half-page magazine

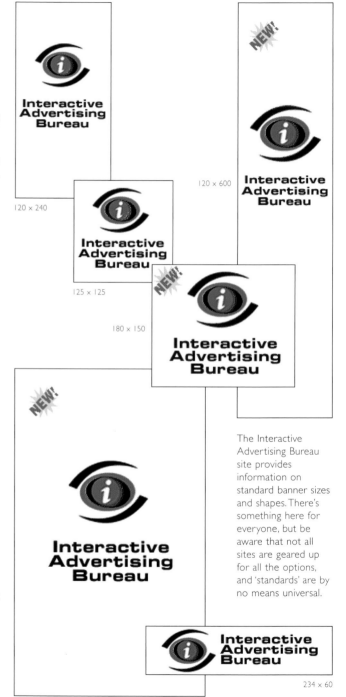

120 × 240

125 × 125

180 × 150

120 × 600

240 × 400

234 × 60

The Interactive Advertising Bureau site provides information on standard banner sizes and shapes. There's something here for everyone, but be aware that not all sites are geared up for all the options, and 'standards' are by no means universal.

18

88 × 31

120 × 60

120 × 90

160 × 600

250 × 250

336 × 280

300 × 250

468 × 60

print ad can easily run to 30MB or more, yet most of today's modems are lucky to muster even 3KB per second in download time. Although your banner ad is small in terms of its dimensions, that doesn't mean it will download quickly enough to pacify impatient website visitors. So, all banner ads have to be designed for swift download, and that means a trade-off between creativity and download time. If your banner doesn't appear quickly on the page, it probably won't be seen as the user scrolls down.

Of course, a good designer always sees a nightmare as a challenge. The format has sparked some ingenious and creative solutions, often deploying animation to make up what is lost in eye-catching dimensions. It gives the ad some extra clout. But animation is heavy on file size: each frame means an extra image. However, clever looping and other visual tricks, combined with simple graphics and fine optimization using the GIF format, are usually enough to do the trick. More about this in the next chapter…

19

BANNERS & BUTTONS

Who hates banners?

Still, all this hasn't been enough to stave off a general trend of "banner blindness." At best, many visitors will simply scroll down before your lovingly crafted (and expensive) ad has loaded. At worst, they will be irritated by it and begin associating that irritation with visiting the site. Nothing gets read, nothing gets clicked, no new money gets spent, and the website might actually start to lose traffic.

This bitterness has given rise to a raft of software packages that visitors can use to stop the ads downloading, and in a sense abuse the free service offered by the site.

Fortunately, good business people listen to consumers, and the failure of the banner format to generate serious business, not to mention the bursting of the dot-com bubble, set Web workers thinking about better solutions.

The even humbler button

Ironically, the result was even smaller: the tiny button ad. Clocking in at a miniscule 120 x 60 pixels, 120 x 120 pixels, or more recently 120 x anything, the main purpose of the button was to not look like a banner.

Ideally occupying a column down the right-hand side of the page (close to where your cursor hovers as you read, and near to the scroll bar), button ads have much in common with print classified ads that are sold by the column inch.

They have also, in many cases, been more successful than banners, because users are less likely to scroll past them indignantly (they occupy the same horizontal space as the site's content). Buttons are more likely to catch a wandering eye and a click-through, and from time to time a bit of real business.

Of course, there's still not a lot you can do or say with a 120-pixel-square graphic: after all, we're talking

1

2

3

4

5

6

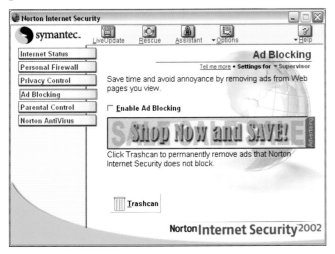

8

about 20 words of solid 11-pixel text and no images, if you're lucky. Stick in a picture, and you might get four words on there (unless you animate the button). But the shape of the space you have to work with is far more conducive to traditional advertising imagery—product shots, models, logos, and so on—and the proximity of the ad to something your target viewer is already looking at reduces the need to "shout."

The skyscraper

So, the button is an improvement, but really only an incremental one. Big advertisers like big spaces, and big spaces attract big money. Clients like these want to dominate and not share a space. They certainly don't want to be halfway down a column of 15 wriggling, GIF-animated buttons all vying for a stray click.

The solution? Bring on the skyscraper! It's a true king in the field of standard banners and buttons. 120 pixels wide at standard, it's effectively a piece of button real estate grown large, and stretched long enough to take up a full first fold of the screen and more. In print terms, it's a full-column ad.

GIF animation is out for skyscrapers—you'll never get it to download quickly enough. You'll also have to be extra clever with your graphics and compression to get the ad down to a decent file size while still retaining image quality. On the plus side, though, the space you get to play with is a luxury.

You can deliver multiple messages that are revealed as your user scrolls. You can fit five black and white photos top to toe, and you can really develop an identity that makes a mark on the page.

In fact, it's suprising that the skyscraper is relatively new on the scene. But the trend is catching on, and the ads often deliver the results to match their stature. Online advertising may, temporarily perhaps, breathe a sigh of relief.

21

1 | 2 | 3
All major sites that accept banners offer guidelines on how to position them and about what formats are accepted. They may also be specific about maximum file sizes for each

different format. If you want something different, don't be afraid to ask: many of these sites are keen to get whatever business they can. All sizes are in pixels: this is a cast-iron rule.

4 | 5 | 6
The flexible shape of the button allows for different positioning in a variety of settings. The choice of shape depends on the message being delivered.

7 | 8
Lots of software exists that allows users to block banners—thankfully for advertisers only a minority of users stop banner access.

VISUALS OR TEXT?

GIFs and JPEGs

Online adverts have traditionally been simple Web graphics files, created and compressed in the same way as a site logo or a webpage photo, using an application like Photoshop, ImageReady, or Fireworks.

The adverts are typically in one of two file formats, geared toward reducing the file size so they download quickly: GIF or JPEG. Broadly, the GIF format is better for graphics with crispy edges and relatively few colors. The JPEG format is better for photos and softer images, as it reduces file size by reducing detail and crispness.

GIF is clearly the Web advertiser's favorite. It offers animation and transparency, it can achieve smaller files against simple graphics, and at high compression the results tend to look better—especially on text.

The maximum number of colors you can have in any GIF file is 256, or 255 plus transparency, but the final file size drops dramatically as you divide your color count in factors of two. In most Web ad work you should be looking to use a maximum of 32, or maybe even as few as eight. The sooner your ad appears on the page, the more clicks you will get.

Animated GIFs are a sequence of pictures put in order to create the illusion of movement. This is the simplest way to make banners "achieve standout." The main drawback is that each frame makes the file size larger and the download time slower, so designers have to work hard to realize an animation concept within the limitations of the technology.

The limitations can be severe. Yahoo!, for example, only takes sizes up to 18K for banners, and limits the duration of animations, in some cases to just six seconds with no looping. It also often asks for animations to be delayed by six seconds while the page downloads.

The button format is even tougher. Often these have to be as little as 3K in size, which means your message has to be concise and to the point.

Think text

GIFs and towering skyscrapers may rule the roost, but some advertisers are turning away from eye-catching visuals altogether.

It's tempting when you design an ad to really go for it with colors, graphics, logos, photos, flashing messages—in fact, anything to grab attention. But what if there's a much better way to attract not just the viewer's eye, but also their interest?

Clearly, some sites have to look good—they're after a stylish audience—and if you're advertising on a site like this, then you need to satisfy the audience's requirements if they're the people your client wants to reach. This might mean clean, minimal, and sophisticated for an upmarket fashion site, or busy, street-smart, and colorful for, say, a skateboard, hip hop, or dance music site.

But that's not all that the Web's about. At least as many sites—probably many, many more—are there simply to supply information for the viewer to browse and pull off when they find it. Here, style comes last in a list of priorities that includes speed, accessibility, and ease of use. Think of Google, Yahoo!, The Washington Post, and so on.

1 | 2
Most major sites, such as AltaVista and Google, carry information for advertisers that describe what formats and sizes are available and how they might best be used.

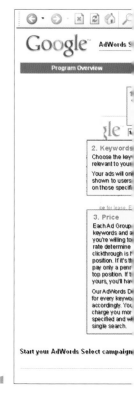

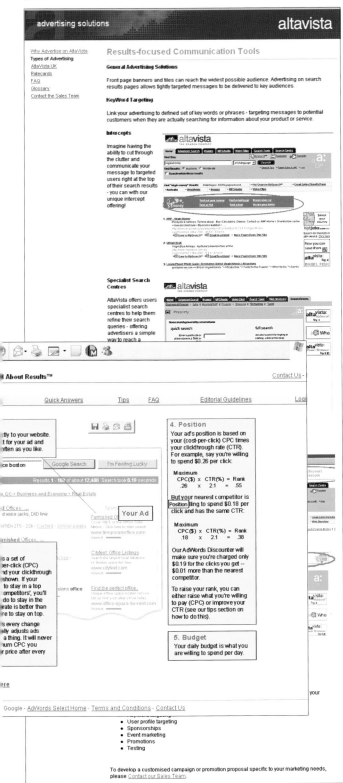

If you want to place a successful ad here, surely you should be looking to gel with what the audience is after, or follow the philosophy that brings them to the site in the first place? If you don't, aren't you missing the point?

Increasingly, you'll see ads that use simple, static text graphics with well-crafted wording to get the message across; or simple HTML-formatted text, which loads far quicker than graphics files and slots easily into the flow of content.

On Google, you'll find the idea taken to a logical extreme. Here, the favored ad format is a plain, design-free text box that looks like a search result. It loads fast, it's says what it means, and it maintains the no-frills ethos of the site.

Matchmakers

There's more to this than a few lines of text, however.

Perform any search on Google and a series of small boxes appear that contain text links to a site that you might find of interest (based on your search). Search for "Olympic games," for example, and these boxes will be populated with links to sportswear retailers or other related sites.

These advertisements work purely on text and keyword relationships. The browser compares the words the user has typed in against the advertiser's preselected keywords, after which the browser is programed to decide whether the user wants to see the ad or not—in other words whether there is a suitable match between the user and the advertiser.

So while on the surface the ads look simple, the technology that actually drives them and matches them to what users want is relatively sophisticated—and it works. If your advertisement only appears to your target audience, the chances of a successful match between seller and buyer are that much higher.

23

INTERACTIVE ADS

The text advertisements on Google are functional advertisements, in that they respond to what the user is interested in.

But you don't need Google to run this type of campaign. If you want to create a text ad that lists your top ten bestselling products in plain text, on a well-targeted site with users that match your target audience, this should work just as well.

You can format the text, apply colors to match your branding, a small logo, and even a 40 pixel-square product shot. The text will still appear instantly on the page, as the graphics download.

For some time now clever advertisers have been taking this type of HTML ad to the next level, including a simple form within their allocated space. This could be just a search box and a "go" button—very popular with Web hosts saying "Find out now if your domain name (site address) is free"—or a dropdown menu of key product categories you have to offer. The user makes a selection, and is whisked off to the relevant page.

Shhh...

Sometimes it is better just to be quiet, and listen. Users love the opportunity to provide their own input, and form elements are eminently clickable. If you have a substantial range of products to promote, your ad could present a complete product finder, with the message, "Find me something that does this." It's not that hard to set up if you have a data-driven website, and with a little subtle branding thrown in, you're magnifying your chances of a click with each and every user who sees the advertisement.

This should come as no surprise. The Web can't realistically offer advertisers full-blown graphics and lots of space to do their thing, but what it can offer is interactivity. That is the crux of the medium, and it is also what it does best.

1

2

Traditional online advertising has been about getting a click-through to the site, where the real sales work can begin, because advertisers worry they can't do justice to their product in a small space.

But this is to misunderstand what is possible, and what users want. They don't want to click on an ad only to be sold something—they need to be already sold on the idea before they click, and the page following this simply delivers the result. This is what an interactive ad achieves: by making a selection and clicking the "go" button, your user has been able to speak, not just listen, and the advertiser is able to deliver a result.

4

5

3

1 | 2 | 3
In the three examples here, pop-ups, one of the most complained-about ad formats on the Web, have been used with varying degrees of success. The John Lewis pop-up takes someone browsing the partner site Handbag.com straight to a related service.

Similarly, the AOL pop-up is advertising an update to its service, which will be of direct interest to AOL users.

The third pop-up, however, bears little relevance to the screen content—it's out of context.

4 | 5 | 6
This lack of context is one of the most annoying aspects of pop-ups.

Get smart

While Google's plain text and other HTML ads tend (but don't need) to be simple in design, other advertisers see things differently—often the sort of advertisers where it's style or entertainment that drives the brand. But the same sophisticated interactivity and functionality remain the staple in what are called "smart ads" (*see page 17*).

Speed of connection, faster servers and better technologies have meant that a large variety of new formats have been developed. The last few years has seen the emergence of interstitials (pages between pages); pop-ups (small windows that pop up above the webpage being viewed); superstitials (polite pop-ups that load after pages have loaded and been viewed); and other new formats. There has also been an emergence of highly interactive formats. These make use of Flash and DHTML, and can provide quite interesting experiences.

The Interactive Advertising Bureau trade group, Microsoft, and DoubleClick released research in 2001 which suggested that highly interactive, larger-format ads had the greatest impact. Although it is good to feel reassured by research, it is no great surprise that a flock of birds flying across a page will attract your attention, if nothing else. Likewise, if you roll your mouse over an ad and something appears from within, it is also likely that your attention will be guaranteed for a moment. The downside, though, is the annoyance factor.

Someone wanting to view content and finding their ability to do so being hindered by your campaign might form a very negative impression about the brand (and the website). Pop-ups, in particular, have come in for heavy criticism: users complain about the number of extra windows they have to manage when all they want to do is read the latest weather report.

In any discussion of ad formats, the watchword has got to be context. The right message in the right format at the right time will always work. It's as simple as that.

25

BRAND AWARENESS

Perhaps the major issue for businesses online is brand awareness: after all, this is what brought down many a dot-com after the heady days of the Internet boom.

Online and in the wider digital space, creating brand awareness is still a relatively new game. But companies are rapidly discovering that intrusive advertising— campaigns that aim to fill every available space and click with a "sell" message—can do untold damage to a brand, and to the host website. Advertisers are rapidly coming to accept that new thinking is the key to making new media work, and that "old media" rules should not be applied to an environment that has its own unique characteristics and rules.

There have been many campaigns to get simple banners removed from the Web, and there are several freely available software packages (in freeware or shareware versions) that stop banners and other ad forms from loading. On the face of it, many of these campaigns are orchestrated by purists and online campaigners. But take a cursory look at just about any Web forum (outside marketing-based ones, of course), and you will find many people complaining about pop-ups and interstitials.

Non-intrusive, sensitively placed ads do not receive such a bad press, however. In fact, just as TV adverts are often more popular than the programmes, the best ads sometimes get forwarded via email. This is one of the Web's unique advantages over other media: once the ball has been set rolling, campaigns can be self-perpetuating and promoted by potential customers at zero cost. Designing campaigns that appeal to the online community is an art worth learning; get it right and you could create a viral marketing phenomenon (*see page 106*).

26

1 | 2 | 3
Handbag.com accepts sections that are sponsored by appropriate brands. This operates in exactly the same way as TV sponsorship.

4 | 5 | 6
Amazon is one site that uses service as a branding tool. If a customer registers they can choose to have the site personalized, so they are greeted as a unique, individual customer with unique and individual tastes. Sponsorship and other traditional techniques are also prevalent.

A classic example of this was a John West Salmon ad that was a short film of a fisherman fighting a bear for its salmon catch. The link to this footage was a hit worldwide. In terms of brand awareness, the campaign's impact was extremely high: higher, in fact, than the media planners had intended.

Another way in which brand awareness is tackled is through building a service culture to match the brand's stated values.

More than ever before, the way a website and customer interact can determine the brand's level of success. Amazon, the online retailer, has a very high and positive brand awareness due in no small part to the high level of customer service. The site functions well, and it is easy to search for, find, and buy a product: the service matches Amazon's aims and its business model. That is Amazon's brand proposition.

From this we can infer that the more complex and illogical an interactive website or advertising campaign is, the less people will like it or respond to it. It pays to think of the interaction as a conversation, a dialog. Follow the rules of polite conversation and no one will be offended. Too much advertising on the Web, alas, does not follow the rules of polite conversation.

Digital branding has become increasingly prevalent through sponsorship of content. As with television, a link-up with the right content can be a very effective branding tool. This has recently been taken further into the realms of content creation by advertisers. Certain large brands have started to take direct control of content on the Web. Many businesses are now producing newsletters, games, and other content to enhance their brand across the digital space.

Brand messages are increasingly becoming tied up with the nature of the interactivity rather than the visuals. How a site "feels" to a user can make or break a brand message.

DOMAINS

Early in the history of the Web there was a scramble to register domain names in the "land grab" for territory in the new digital world. These are the addresses that are typed into a browser to take you to a site. There were many tales of small companies or individuals buying potential domain names of major corporations with the express intention of selling them at a profit.

The value of a Web domain can be enormous to a brand. With many companies, users can simply guess at the "com" version of the company name and go straight to the site. This means that the owner of the domain will get the traffic it requires, so owning the "right" domain is highly important.

Modern browsers also allow users to type shortened addresses into the address bar for larger brands and the browser will find the site. This ease of searching means that a brand or company can stand head and shoulders above other companies in terms of hits on their site.

1 | 2 | 3

Most major brands control domain names tightly across the world. Coca-Cola is just one company that makes great use of the worldwide nature of the Web, owning domains across all major territories.

2

3

28

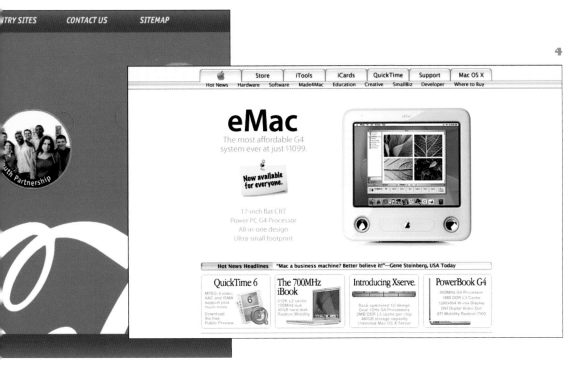

4 | 5
Apple Computer is another corporation that makes good use of worldwide domains. Compare its US site with its Japanese site and it is clearly the same, but each appears in their respective local language. In this way the company projects exactly the same brand values across the world.

29

DOMAIN NAMES

There are so many sites out there based on businesses with similar names that differentiation is crucial. Given the number of people in the world with the name "McDonald," it is clear that the burger chain would be interested in owning the domain name and others similar to it. It is rumored that the actor Arnold Schwarzenegger bought up all the common misspellings of his name and typing in any of them will take the user to his main site. True or not in this case, this is something that many large corporations have done.

The owning of domain names is also important when relying on users finding the site through a search engine. The bigger the brand, the higher up the results they will want to appear. In combination with keywords, having a range of similar domain names can help the brand climb higher up the rankings.

The main argument driving this ownership is that owning a domain name is the same as owning a copyright trade name. Although exempt from legislation initially, buying up domain names with the specific intention of reselling them has in recent years been frowned upon. Courts around the world are increasingly taking the view that a domain name is as much a part of a corporate identity as the name on a storefront or product.

30

2

1

3

4

7

1 | 2 | 3 | 4 | 5
McDonald's, Disney, Visa, and other worldwide brands adopt similar working practices. This applies even when the same company has different local names.

6 | 7
Exxon/Esso: with care they can convey the same values to all territories.

DOMAINS—FURTHER USES

As we have seen, domain names have become an integral part of a corporate ID and brand experience. They have, however, also begun to be used directly as marketing tools.

It is worth explaining here what a domain name is. A domain name is a URL (Uniform Resource Locator) which in turn is a written version of a series of numbers that describes where a computer is on the Internet.

This address written out simply can act as a very efficient way of getting consumers to a site where they can be given the full advertising message. Advertisers have been swift to take advantage of this. It is now a central part of marketing campaigns to purchase promotion-specific domain names. The motor company BMW has done this very successfully with its microsite www.bmwfilms.com, a site that exists solely to promote the brand through the creation of unique content. This site is not linked to the company's main corporate site.

Specialist sites

Many advertisers have taken this route in recent years. Seasonal sales have been promoted via microsites with specific domain names. The rise in promotional interactive games has also fuelled the domain name rush, as has the film industry, which uses specialist domain names for each major launch. www.starwars.com is one of the biggest and is constantly used to promote the new films and related merchandising as well as acting as a community for fans. Every release now carries a separate domain name. Just a few years ago, they were sub-directories of the main film company site. It is clear that it becomes easier for consumers to remember a film title than a long extended sub-directory. In a nutshell, that's the marketing appeal of a domain name, and partly explains why major films are often developed "under wraps" so information can't leak out to hostile parties.

In terms of branding online, the domain name is the starting point; everything else follows on from that.

1

3

1 | 2
Both starwars.com and bmwfilms.com are successful examples of corporations and companies owning domain names related to one particular product range or marketing initiative.

3 | 4 | 5
bmwfilms.com contains specially commissioned film content whereas starwars.com is intended to act as a focus of the promotional activities surrounding each new episode of the saga.

4

5

FURTHER FORMATS

The earlier part of this chapter talked about the top level of issues surrounding formats and ad types. We have also looked at domain names, branding and microsites. But there are numerous other forms of digital advertising.

In the last two or three years there has been an explosion of online games. As the effectiveness of "traditional" online formats has been called into question, advertisers have looked for other formats to extend their reach and develop their brands online. Games have often been the solution: give customers something to play with or against, and they will swiftly forget they are interacting with an advertisement.

Consumers are better disposed toward advertising when it offers something in return for their time and involvement. From humble "lotto"-style games to complex sports simulations, gambling, and gaming—all are a huge growth area—indeed, such advertising may hold the key to the success of future generations of mobile services.

Sticky content

"Content sites" have also become a favoured marketing tool. Brands such as Kellogg's have created sites with "sticky" content to draw users into an ongoing dialog. As mentioned on page 32, bmwfilms.com has been particularly successful in this.

HTML emails are another popular format. These are essentially "designed" emails, similar to webpages, which can be sent out to consumers' inboxes. They can hold forms and links to draw the user into a dialog.

Rich media, video, and audio streams are also expanding as Internet connections become faster. It is now routine for film trailers to be distributed via the Web as promotional tools: teaser trailers for film series such as *Harry Potter* and *Star Wars* are massively popular and drive huge amounts of traffic to parent sites.

1–8
In general, surfers have become accustomed to expecting ever more innovative and media-rich advertising formats.

The MTV example here combines interactivity, Web, phone, and karaoke to provide a compelling and fun proposition that appeals directly to its core audience, and communicates MTV's brand values.

It also clearly demonstrates the potential for newer, richer formats and highlights the drift towards advertiser-produced content.

34

Digital Interactive TV has taken off in several countries and there is now a burgeoning industry surfacing around advertising on this format, too.

The emergence of digital mobile phone systems has also led to advertising being adapted to suit the various formats, from SMS messaging to WAP and i-Mode. Personal Digital Assistants, or PDAs, are particularly popular with business executives, so advertising targeted to this market will find something of a captive audience.

35

WHAT TO PUT IN YOUR AD?

The first, and perhaps most important, task in designing any advert is to decide what to put in it. This might sound obvious, but if you dive straight in with graphics and technologies, but with only a half-baked idea to hinge them on, you will end up wasting your time.

All the best adverts have at their heart a "Really Good Idea," and if this shines through then you can easily overcome the technical limitations of online advertising, such as file size and space. Your idea could be an unforgettable tagline, a visual theme that sears straight to the heart of what a product has to offer, or a simple tale with an entertaining twist.

Your advert doesn't need to be deep or complex to work—after all, many of the most memorable (and therefore successful) traditional adverts carry only a simple message. The same rules apply just as strongly—perhaps even more so—in the online environment.

The more your ad is fighting for attention on a busy webpage, the more important its simplicity and attractiveness becomes. Unlike their television counterparts, people rarely go to websites to look at the ads: they want information, and they want it fast. You need, therefore, to grab their attention instantly, or to entice them enough to pause and take a look.

1 | 2
Wherever an advert is positioned, it has to fight to be seen. Often the more straightforward the message and the clearer the design, the more chance there is of "standout" from the surrounding clutter. In this case both message and design are clear and communicate their intent well.

3
This ad communicates a message by making a virtue of the fact that people use notes to remind themselves what to do.

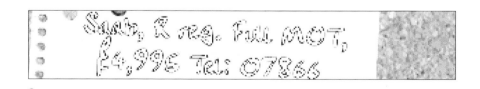

2

3

4

Typically, an advert is made up of images—either photography or illustration—text, which is known as copy, and a logo. It's not that big a limitation: after all, that's about all the print advertiser has to play with, bar perhaps a stick-on product sample.

The TV advertiser, of course, can factor sound, a good script, and movement into the equation, to create a mini-movie. The Internet offers all of these; and although you may never achieve the same crisp image quality and smooth animation online, online medium

does boast a "killer app" that makes it a unique medium for the creative thinker: interactivity.

If you consider advertising as the beginning of a conversation, where the interactive ad can only respond if the viewer wants to join in, then the opportunity for offering entertainment, choice, and a more fulfilling advertising experience becomes clear. Through skillful, creative thinking and design, the interactive ad can hold viewers' attention for far longer, and increase your chances of a click in the right place.

Whatever ingredients you decide to use, they need to achieve a number of things in a short space of time. They need to attract attention, say what the product or service is, say who's offering it, sell a benefit, and then tell the viewer what to do about it. This is the classic "call to action" of advertising, and it applies more online than elsewhere.

In the case of some online ads using interactive features, the benefit and call to action may be the ad itself. Take, for example, a search box advertisement offering a quick and convenient way to find out if your preferred domain name is free. In more traditional cases, the objective could be to communicate why one particular product is better than others, to lodge a brand name in surfers' minds, or in many cases, simply to get people to click through to another page where the real pitch begins.

To achieve all of this within the confines of a 468 x 60 pixel banner, a 120 x 450 skyscraper, or even a 500 x 400 microsite, creates the need for a lean and effective idea. There is simply no room for fluff.

39

4 | 5
Both adverts use simple text, images and design to communicate.

CHOOSING FORMATS AND MEDIA

You have the concept for your campaign. Now what? It's wise before you press on with design work to pin down which formats, media, and file types you'd like to use. These may be specified by a client or closely tied in with your "Really Good Idea." They will also determine how you approach the design and production to get maximum effect within the environment—and that vitally swift download.

For example, an ad banner must fight for attention within a webpage, and get a message across quickly. A microsite on the other hand can offer users more in-depth information and entertainment. On another level, the type of graphics that are effective and speedy in GIF, JPEG, HTML, and Flash formats are quite different in each case, and, accordingly, you need to approach the design in quite a different way for each. Choosing between them can be tough, but you'll thank yourself later if you can do this up front.

Software choice

You need to compare the features that different media have to offer with the objectives you want to reach. We'll explore the intricacies as we go on, but, in short, Flash is ideal for interactivity and fast-loading animation; GIF for plug-in-free, simple animations and readability; JPEG for photographic-style design; and simple HTML for fast-loading, readable text and forms.

The average ad campaign will draw in a range of formats and media, and perhaps use several sets of artwork and copy to convey its message: for example, a couple of banners, buttons, and skyscrapers, a pop-up, a five-page microsite and an email bulletin. The challenge for the designer is to get a single, congruous theme working across the whole project, so that any lay viewer can know instantly that these things belong together.

Some of the chief ways of tying disparate elements together include creating consistent layout and color

schemes, utilizing a family of typefaces, presentation styles, interactive behaviors, and more. We'll look at all of these over the coming pages.

In any campaign, the planners and designers need to work closely together to decide what approach to take in order to best convey the message. Also, it is vital to apply consistency to the campaign. There are two ways to approach this. One is to treat the online campaign as separate. The second, which advertisers are doing increasingly, is to use the online arena to extend offline campaigns.

■ This microsite advertising a movie uses Flash in a pop-up window inviting the user to click. Flash allows a great deal of interactivity if a user just touches an ad.

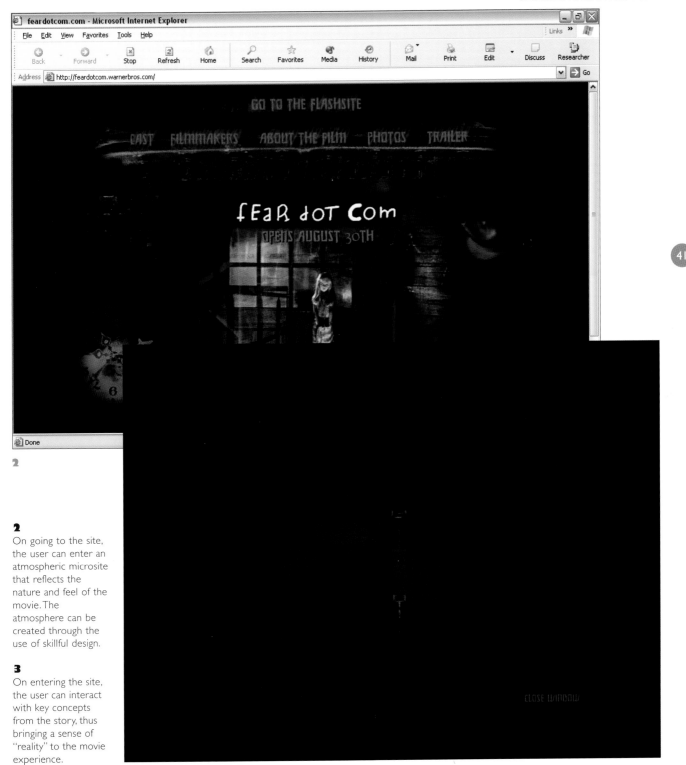

2

2
On going to the site, the user can enter an atmospheric microsite that reflects the nature and feel of the movie. The atmosphere can be created through the use of skillful design.

3
On entering the site, the user can interact with key concepts from the story, thus bringing a sense of "reality" to the movie experience.

3

LOOK & LAYOUT

If you have a good concept for an ad, then much of the rest will follow on naturally from it. It's "just" a matter of translating your ideas into pixels. But the sheer number of options and technicalities the Internet throws at you can make it hard to know where to begin.

The best place to start is with a pencil and paper, rather than a computer. Using these you can quickly sketch out a range of layout ideas, key frames of animation, or interactive events for your various ad formats. If they don't feel right on paper, they probably won't work well in the digital realm either. It's far easier to change your mind at this point than after six hours' work in Photoshop or Flash!

Some details of your ad design will probably have been dictated by the existing brand image for the product or service you're promoting. An established identity can include colors, styling, typefaces, a "language" appropriate to the product, and more.

Mixed media

But the real difficulty in working across a range of formats and media is that all the shapes, spaces, and features are different. With in-page ads like banners, the task inevitably boils down to shoehorning images into a tall or a wide area, then somehow fitting the copy around it. With interstitials (*see page 25*), you're struggling to get anything worth displaying within a tolerable file size.

With small ads, your range of layout options is very limited; the difference between one layout and another may just be where the logo goes and how big the text is. The need for a unique idea to set you apart becomes pressing.

The banner for the mobile phone competition on the first image here is designed to look like content. The layout of the ad echoes the layout of the site on which it is placed. The fonts are similar in size to the headlines from the site itself, and the smaller text reflects the smaller site text. The layout proportions follow the classical idea of division into fifths.

Bear in mind, however, that some types of website—such as specialist news services—discourage or actively forbid advertisements that "masquerade" as authorized content, as the host may not want to appear to "endorse" an advertiser's claims. In the second example, from the Fox Kids website (www.foxkids.com), the host site is a rich visual experience, so the ad layout gives more prominence to the message. It has been designed to sit within a color scheme that contrasts with the host site to set itself apart.

Layouts for pop-ups and other formats follow similar rules, with due consideration to position and context.

3

In this case, the ads are clearly designed to reflect the fact that they are being positioned on a children's site.

2

1
Banners are sometimes designed to look like the content in the pages—a sort of camouflage which can be very useful. There is, however, a disadvantage: users who click on the banner accidentally can resent then seeing an advert.

2
Ads can look very rich and full of life. They may also reflect the fun content of a site, as is clearly the case here. The message can be strengthened by allowing products that have strong associations to be seen alongside other excellent brands.

THE POWER OF PICTURES

There are few better ways to grab attention and get a message across than a really superb image with plenty of space around it. It's true that space may be too much to expect, depending on the site(s) where your adverts are placed. However, you can create a semblance of it with clever design. If you have impressive artwork or photography for a campaign, it's worth paring the other elements down to a bare minimum, and putting them second in the visual pecking order.

44

Why images?

The power of images derives from the fact that people don't need to read pictures. All it takes is a glance, and in that moment the viewer has taken on board a whole story, complete with values and assumptions—hopefully about how good your product is. Moreover, people don't tend to realize they are being sold to in this way, which weakens the barriers of distrust and scepticism.

There is another, simpler, reason to focus on images for adverts on a webpage: they stand out more. Most sites are jam-packed with text, some graphics, and very few iconic images. In particular, you'll see surprisingly few pictures of people on the Web, whereas print and TV marketing people hold dear to their hearts the knowledge that an attractive model can sell just about anything.

There is, however, a problem with images, and this is that they take up a lot of kilobytes. The bigger and more complex your picture is, the longer it will take to download. If the average Web user spends an average of 30 seconds on a webpage (rather than a website) before clicking off somewhere else, and your ad takes 15 seconds to load, then you've only exploited half the exposure available to you. Research clearly suggests that ads that load quicker get more clicks. For those who hold the purse strings, this is more important than looking pretty.

1

2

3

4

The solution is to think carefully about what type of images you want to use, and how effectively they will compress (so that they load quickly but lose as little quality as possible). A small number of flat colors works well as a GIF, and photographic images work well as a JPEG—but the latter offers no animation potential.

Television-style graphics based on photorealism are such a powerful way to convey quality that it comes as no surprise that quality brands are starting to exploit the power of pictures.

ns heads just as quickly

www.bmw.co.uk

1 | 2 | 3 | 4

This advertisement for BMW UK begins with an image that moves fluidly and with a degree of smoothness found in film and television. It then cuts to text to deliver the tagline, which provides a neat pun on the car's performance. Next, we see the product and weblink. Finally, the looping "film" returns, reinforcing a high-quality experience.

TEXT

Almost all ads include some kind of text; most carry at least two or three lines, while pop-ups and microsites can dish out the full story (if it is essential to your campaign). The formats where text presents the greatest design challenges are—no surprises—banners and buttons. Again this is simply to do with the available space. But don't be fooled into thinking that more space (at higher cost!) is the solution to a cluttered design, because you can bet your bottom dollar that if a client pays for a bigger ad, they'll simply want more text on it.

This issue crops up throughout Web design, whatever it is that you're designing. Are the words easy to read? In many ads, you don't just want the words to be readable: you want them to SHOUT!

Using capitals is certainly the easy solution, and any text under ten points really needs to be in upper case to be readable. At seven points or less there just aren't enough pixels to properly create the letter forms. But don't despair if small is the only answer to a difficult brief: there are a number of specialist fonts specifically designed to be readable at small sizes, such as the

excellent eight-point Silkscreen, which you can download for free from www.myfonts.com. These types of fonts are called bitmap fonts—they specify the exact pixels to be used to create a letter shape, trading smoothness for tighter control. As a side note, serif fonts are far harder to read on screen at small sizes.

4

3

2

1

46

1 | 2 | 3 | 4

The ads presented here show that clear, legible text can be effective as the sole element in an ad. Using animated text in a range of sizes conveys the message clearly and effectively. The whole tagline about getting smarter is reinforced by the use of words which themselves are indicative of education and cleverness. On a site that has large amounts of text, this style of ad can be very powerful.

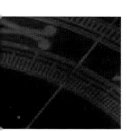

Depending on how much text you want to use in an advertisement, readability and small type will almost certainly be an issue you have to deal with. But to create an uncluttered, accessible design that shouts above all the other advertisments on the same webpage, you also need to make key text elements stand out—usually by making them bigger.

You also need to be aware of the process called anti-aliasing, which softens the curves of letters by shading the edges with mid-tones (that fall between the text and background colors). This make letters more attractive, but increases the file size of a GIF and makes smaller type harder to read. Your design software should allow you to turn it on and off.

COLOR

Generous lashings of bright color are bound to attract the eye, while subtler, blended tones can lend class and restraint to a design. Often a color scheme will be laid down by an existing brand identity; many products are recognizable instantly by the color combinations they use—Coca-Cola, Orange, and FedEx, for example, are all easily identifiable from their corporate colors.

But if this isn't the case, the colors you choose must gel with the image you want to project. If strong imagery is a starting point for your ad design, it's common to use colors eye-dropped (sampled) directly from the image, to ensure the final artwork functions as a whole and does not dazzle the user unnecessarily.

Color also has a direct connection with download time and the file formats you use, which is a good reason to settle on file formats before you settle on a color scheme. The file size of a GIF grows in proportion to the number of precise tones it contains, in steps of 2, 4, 8, 16, 32, and so on up to 256, which is the maximum. Every JPEG offers a complete 16.7 million colors, but you lose crispness of detail in the compression process. This looks particularly poor on aliased text.

If you're a fan of color, you might be tempted to always use JPEGs. This, however, would be a mistake, as GIFs almost always result in clearer, brighter colors. (JPEGs have reduced detail and tend to get muddy around the edges). For even the most sophisticated color scheme, eight tones out of a possible 256 will usually be enough. In fact, if you treat the color reduction process as a creative tool rather than as an obstacle, then you can achieve some really stylish effects with two- or four-color visuals and tiny file sizes. The problem is also the solution.

49

1 | 2 | 3
All the examples shown here demonstrate that making the most of the surroundings helps greatly in creating a successful ad. By showing sensitivity to the context of the ad, your design can have much greater impact. All three examples carry banner ads that are clearly designed to fit into the color scheme of the host page.

BACKGROUNDS

Background images are the ideal solution to many problems in Web design, particular where file size is critical (which is most of the time!).

Take the case of an animated GIF banner. When designing such an ad banner, there is a limit to the file size, yet multiple frames still have to be crammed into the animation. This means that the best way of reducing file size is to work very carefully with the backgrounds. If the background hardly changes, the file size is kept down because the GIF is re-using the same image components.

All decent GIF animation software offers you the option to designate particular layers or graphical elements as part of a static background image.

Remember also that the GIF format supports 100 percent transparency (but not semi-transparency), which allows a webpage background to show through. However, this can look messy if you don't take care to match anti-aliased edges properly.

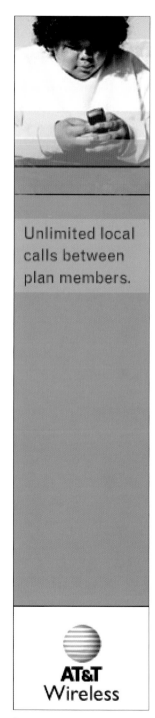

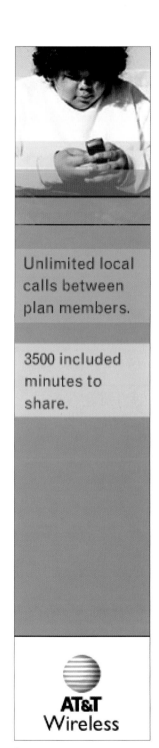

1   2

Unlimited local
calls between
plan members.

3500 included
minutes to
share.

All on one
calling plan
with one bill.

3

Unlimited local
calls between
plan members.

3500 included
minutes to
share.

All on one
calling plan
with one bill.

**AT&T
SHARED
ADVANTAGE**

learn more

4

The background images also make it possible to create artwork in HTML, which makes for a faster download and easier editing. Often in Web design you will want to run text over part of an image, and it is tempting to create the whole lot as a GIF or JPEG to get the styling right. But if you're willing to relax your control a little, using HTML with the finer features of Cascading Style Sheets, or CSS as they are commonly referred to, to place the image as a background with live text running over it is a much better bet.

This technique is becoming increasingly popular with email ads, pop-ups and microsites, where you're usually aiming to deliver a lot of information in an attractive design, but where speed remains critical. Remember: Web users are keen to close pop-ups and delete unknown emails before they even load. Getting something to appear five seconds faster could make the difference of a thousand clicks.

51

1 | 2 | 3 | 4
These skyscrapers
use both photos and
simple backgrounds
to great effect.

PREPARING ADS FOR THE WEB

Images in ads are almost always one of two types, GIF and JPEG. These are the standard Web image formats, and are universally recognized and interpreted by Web browsers. Both include sophisticated features for compressing, or optimizing, graphics to reduce the file size (and therefore the download time). The savings are significant. A photo set to 50% JPEG compression in Fireworks may be 1/8 of the original file size, while a GIF reduced from 256 colors to just two may download at more than 10 times the speed.

Editing and creating images can be done very cheaply. Most designers use Adobe Photoshop (www.adobe.com), Macromedia Fireworks (www.macromedia.com) and other similar packages as they offer unrivalled image control and manipulation potential. There are, however, cheaper alternatives, such as Paint Shop Pro, available as shareware from www.jasc.com, and Adobe's cut-down Photoshop

Elements. All these packages are good, and while for heavy, professional use you'll almost certainly need to pay for the fully-featured packages, in other cases the mid-level options will do you just fine.

Macromedia's Flash package is the standard for creating Flash-format media, and offers incredibly sophisticated tools for doing it. But you'll be in at the deep end if you've never worked with Flash before, and there is an increasing number of third-party apps designed to make the job easier—try SWiSH, which focuses on text effects, for starters, or Swift 3D, which specializes in striking 3D Flash.

Any type of HTML ad—microsites, pop-ups, emails, and so on—can be prepared using ordinary authoring software, like Macromedia's Dreamweaver or HomeSite, and Adobe's GoLive. You create them in exactly the same way as you create any other webpage. Any particulars should be given to you in a client brief or by the carrier of the advertising.

Flash is now heavily used because it is so powerful and has an ease of use that belies this. It also is vector-based, which makes file sizes remain small.

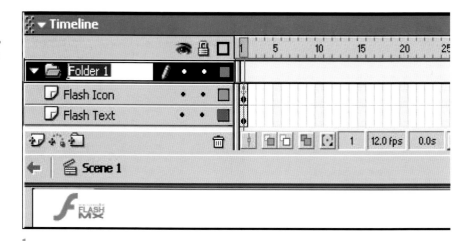

52

2
PaintShopPro is another tool that can be used to create web graphics. This is popular as it retails at a cheap price but has many powerful features.

3
Tools such as SWiSH allow designers to manipulate specific things, in this case text in Flash, in a way that allows more control than the standard tools.

3

ANIMATION

The human eye alerts us to movement easily. On a webpage, if something moves, the visitor will focus on it immediately.

Clearly, animation is a strong tool for attracting attention, especially on a busy page or one that has several ads running simultaneously. In a game it's essential, of course, and in larger formats such as superstitials (*see page 25*) it is also effective to create movement.

Animated banners are usually in animated GIF format. This is a GIF format that can contain numerous cels, just like a traditional animation. What is appealing about this format is that there are many animated GIF creation tools available for next to no cost.

By using the same color background and just changing the foreground, small file sizes can be attained even with tens of frames in the animation. Most sites allow animated GIFs to be displayed, but some specify strict limitations, such as one loop, or a maximum of six frames. This, again, is purely to keep file sizes down, efficiency up, and to reduce visitors' irritation. However, you can make an effective and eye-catching ad even with only one loop and a small number of frames. As a result, most banners are now animated, so the gauntlet has well and truly been thrown down to your creativity.

Flash animation

More advanced animation usually involves using Flash. Because Flash has multiple channels, animations can be made with sophisticated effects that can be synchronized to sound. Flash is a powerful animation tool and does require experience and patience to get the best out of it.

In general, only change what is necessary on each frame. Not only is this good for making economical file sizes, it is also a professional technique that reduces errors. The more you change in a cel, the greater the margin for error.

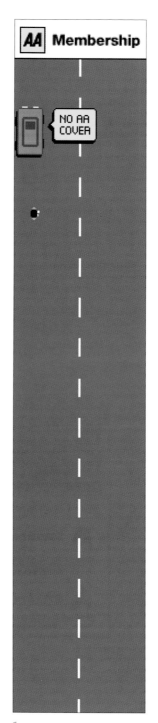

1

2

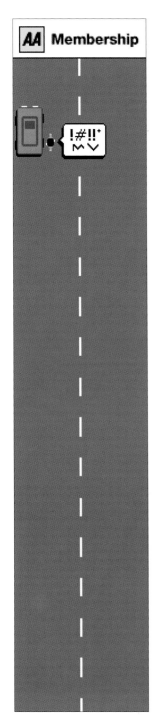

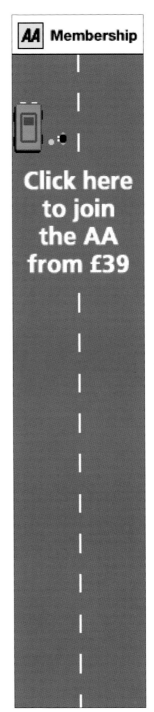

1 | 2 | 3 | 4 | 5
The animated banners here use simple-looking animation to achieve standout on a crowded page. They shout the loudest on a "noisy" page.

55

ROLLOVERS

Rollovers are a very effective way of drawing attention to an ad—as long as people make use of them. As people surf the Web they generally move their mouse around the screen. A rollover banner will react when the mouse touches it. This will normally trigger a change of image or a new message. For example, a banner might change its text when rolled over by the mouse. Because this happens when the user is making the mouse move, their attention is drawn to both the cursor movement and to the rollover effect.

Another reason for using rollovers is to simulate mechanical button actions and create the feeling of maximum response and interactivity. This technique says to the user, click on this and we will take you somewhere and show you something.

Most rollovers on banners are created in JavaScript. This is a language that sits inside HTML, but which is much more powerful, and allows you to create functions like rollovers both quickly and easily. It also helps keeps file sizes down. Coding in JavaScript is not as easy as in HTML but it isn't difficult within the overall scheme of programming languages. Anyone can learn enough to create rollovers and other effects fairly swiftly.

Of course, JavaScript isn't the only tool that makes for easy rollovers, Flash does it too, as does its sister technology, Shockwave. Both of these packages have ready-made rollover functions, which means that there is no need for hand coding. Flash ads can make full use of this power. Flash rollovers, in particular, provide a smooth effect and respond well.

1

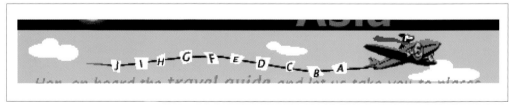

2

3

The downside of rollovers is simple: the user may never trigger the effect because they don't roll the mouse over it. This is where straight animated adverts win out. The decision is yours: rollovers put the user in control and force them to interact, while animation will attract their attention regardless of whether or not they want it to.

As the speed of downloading increases and the number of broadband connections goes up, the use of rollovers has become so much easier that it is developing into a highly usable technique. In terms of conveying a message, the fact that something is revealed when it is touched is a very powerful way of encouraging someone to look more closely at the ad and pay attention to what it has to say.

1 | 2 | 3 | 4 | 5
The images shown here are sample banners from Lycos, but they do show that JavaScript can be used to create rolling banners that are triggered by the mouse rolling over them, as well as interactive banners.

5

4

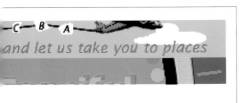

INTERACTIVITY

Looking at text, color, backgrounds, images, and so on, and examining the ads that are out there can only lead to one conclusion: that adverts in general are becoming increasingly interactive.

Faster downloads, DHTML, JavaScript and Flash, plus the increased sophistication of users, have combined to create a scenario where full interactivity is both possible and desirable.

When a user can begin to play with a simple banner and, for example, perform a search via the banner, then some of the potential of digital advertising is starting to be realized. There are now many humble banners that carry games, or allow a user to search for music and videos. Using a combination of all these techniques for different scenarios means you never need to create a dull, static banner again. Designers feel that interactive ads provide an easy route for the consumer to access a service, or engage more fully with a sales message.

By creating interactive ads, the advertiser is beginning to use the potential of the medium. As discussed earlier, ad text can be updated in real time, and ads can also be used as search engines. In short, they can allow a brand to reach out and touch the consumer, or invite the consumer to make contact with the brand. Interactivity is akin to dialog, and this is increasingly what consumers demand of a company. Your competitors may offer a dialog, which means your customers will also demand it of you.

To the consumer it must seem as natural as having a normal conversation and in common with a normal conversation, there has to be a form of reply.

Games and Flash movies use interactivity heavily. In fact, it is difficult to see how a non-interactive game would work. This interactivity is a strong part of the story a brand tells about itself, and it needs designing as much as a simple graphic does.

1 | 2 | 3 | 4 | 5
The ads shown here all use levels of interactivity to draw the consumer into a dialog. As they rub away the "paper," the message is revealed.

1

3

2

4

59

5

6

SOUND

This is one of the trickiest elements of design, and one of the least used. This is because, first, it is hard to compress sound down to an acceptable file size for the Web, and second, people don't often have the sound on their computers switched on at work (and if they do, noisy adverts would quickly make them switch it off!).

Sound files are notoriously difficult to compress because they have to carry a lot of digital information to produce sounds accurately. The ear is not easily fooled by poor quality sound.

Common sound formats include WAV, AIFF, and to some extent, AU. But none of these offer adequate compression and cross-platform support to make them realistic options. MP3 (the compression format that became a lifestyle statement), RealAudio, and QuickTime have become dominant in the field, with Windows Media (or WMF) catching up. All four of these offer streaming, which enables a track to begin playing before it has completed loading; but all also require a plug-in to play.

Flash sound

Most conducive to the ad designer will be Flash format, which has full support for MP3 audio. This means you can add sounds to a Flash movie, and when you export the movie for the Web, your Flash application (or Flash itself) will compress the sound in MP3 format and include it as part of the movie file. You can easily syncronize the sound to various interactive and animation events. Flash

also supports "vector audio," an emerging area pioneered by the British company Sseyo (www.sseyo.com).

Optimizing sound

Sound artists usually perform a range of tricks to bring audio in under a reasonable file size. Trick one is to make the file mono (stereo files are twice as large). Second, the file size can be reduced by reducing the bit depth. This is the audio equivalent of reducing the number of colors in an image. Thirdly, many sound files are looped in advertisements. This means creating only a short clip and reusing it cyclically. Beware, though, that looped sound can be annoying if it is not cleverly used.

Obviously, in games and in Flash movies, you can use much more sound: in the background, for example, or as sound effects accompanying actions.

In spite of all of the above reservations and caveats, there is no doubt that audio really can cut through the clutter and be a powerful call to action.

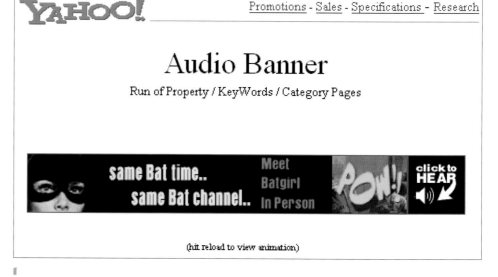

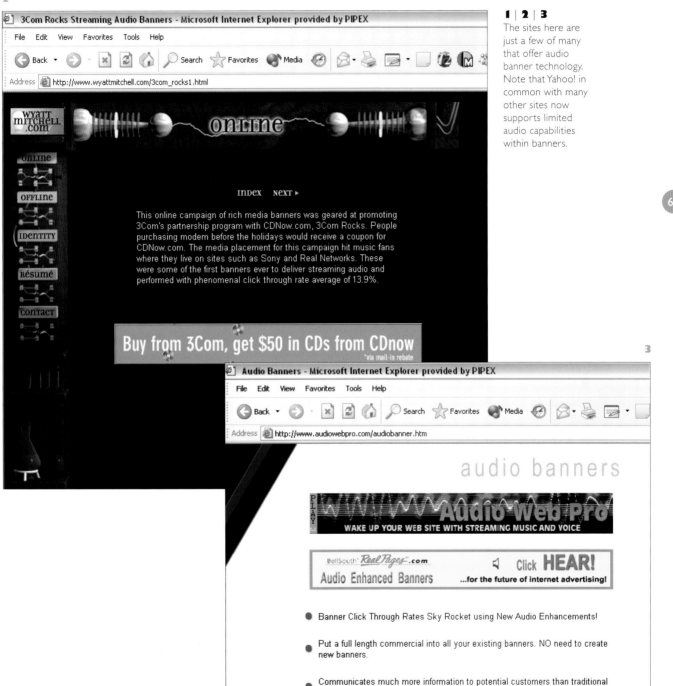

1 | 2 | 3
The sites here are just a few of many that offer audio banner technology. Note that Yahoo! in common with many other sites now supports limited audio capabilities within banners.

VIDEO

Perhaps more of a natural choice than sound for the majority of Internet surfers is video, although the problems you face in compressing sound files acceptably will be multiplied many times over with video. Then there is the cost of putting a video together. Remember also that simply editing video— let alone getting it online—is an art in itself, and will have its own cost implications.

But with the rise of broadband Internet access, improved delivery technologies, and consumer demand for a more entertaining and involving online experience, video has come to play a great role in online marketing—but not yet in banners and buttons. More on this later.

Almost all high-profile film and computer game releases involve a marketing campaign of streaming online trailers, previews, clips, and other similiar types of material. These will often be placed on a microsite, which is promoted using the more old-school GIF, JPEG, and email techniques. There are now a great many sites out there that specialize solely in preview trailers, and viewers are so keen to see them that entire cultures have evolved around them, offering what is, effectively, free advertising.

62

1
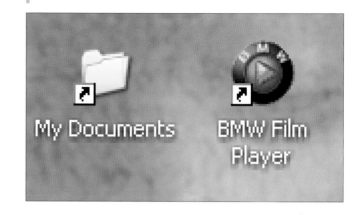

2
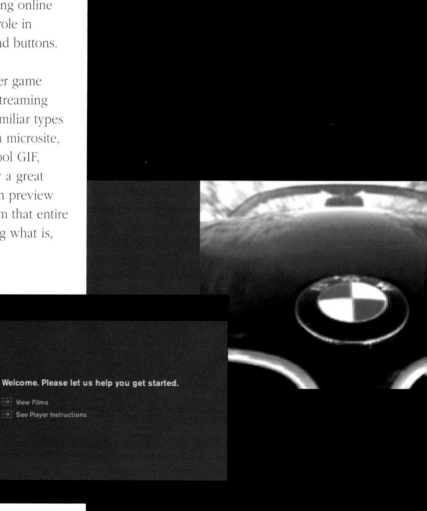

3

BMW ■
Interactive
Film Player v1.0

Welcome. Please let us help you get started.

→ View Films
→ See Player Instructions

1 | 2 | 3 | 4

This superb ad campaign used the full range of latest techniques. The user could download a customized player from which they could view the high-quality short feature films made to show off the values of the product. This approach has also begun to be used by game publishers as their games increasingly take on cinematic values.

If you've got the resources to create a decent trailer, it's well worth it!

The formats you use will typically be the same as for audio, with QuickTime being particularly popular for trailers, and RealMedia, Windows Media, MPEG, and AVI in tow.

From version 6, Flash also natively supports video with impressive compression, and this is likely to spawn a rapid increase in video clips and snapshots directly integrated into interactive banners, pop-ups, and so on. It offers an intuitive new way for designers to work with video, alongside interactive possibilities that other media cannot match.

Video tends to be used for high-quality products at the moment as the buyers of these products are more likely to have fast computers and fast connectivity. Video also conveys film and TV sensibilities and values that differentiate the products from those promoted by hand-drawn or static banners.

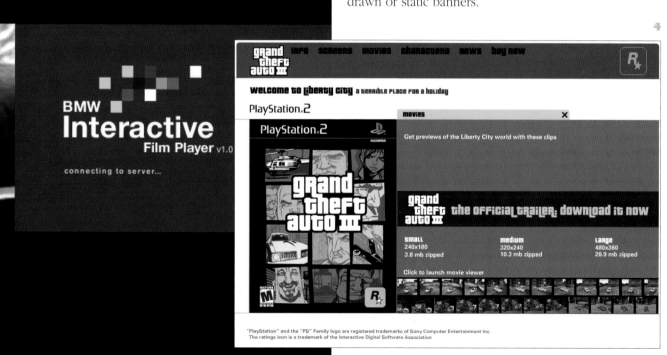

BEYOND THE BANNER

We've discussed a range of online ad formats. But what do they have to offer?

Pop-ups have attracted a great deal of attention from Net heads for all the wrong reasons: they hate them. Advertisers, on the other hand, claim they are extremely effective. So who do you believe? Well, what is certain is that they are often used insensitively, interfering with the online experience and obscuring content. This might get your advertisement noticed, but it certainly won't make users buy your product.

Pop-up or pop-under?

If you use pop-ups sensitively, they can still be made to perform some eye-catching feats. They can shake, move around, and even resize. It might be gimicky, but visitors will certainly notice it. Pop-ups can also be designed to appear as "pop-unders," in that they can appear behind the browser and wait to be seen when the user closes a window. This less obtrusive method is effective, and does not detract from what users want when visiting a website.

In fact, there are standard pop-ups, and there are smart ones. The superstitial is a proprietary format that acts as a polite pop-up. When a page is loaded, the superstitial begins to load. If anything else starts to load it stops. When a user clicks on a link on a page, the superstitial pops up and can be interacted with.

Interstitials take a slightly different approach. These are pages that appear between pages on a site. When a user clicks and goes from one page to the next, the interstitial appears and then disappears when the new page appears. This has also been surprisingly effective.

1 | 2 | 3 | 4
The superstitial works by filling the space between pages that are downloading from a website.

1

2

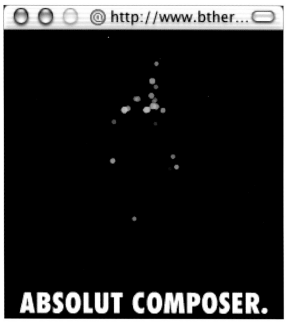

3

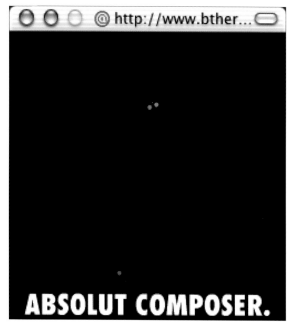

4

Panicware, Inc.

Internet Privacy Solution

Home	Products	Download	Purchase	Support

Pop-Up Stopper®

Panicware is proud to offer **three versions** of our popular Ad Blocking software. Our Pop-Up Stopper Free is completely free for personal use! Want to use Pop-Up Stopper at the office? Try Pro or Companion! Not sure which version is right for you? Click here to compare our products!

More Info...

Supports Internet Explorer 5.x - 6.x
Netscape 4.x - 7.x

Pop-Up Stopper FREE

Basic Ad Blocking for Internet Explorer and Netscape!
Panicware's award winning, completely FREE pop-up and pop-under ad blocking product. Over 4.5 million users can't be wrong - get yours today!

Pop-Up Stopper FREE is not adware or spyware and is free for personal use - no registration required!

Important: Pop-Up Stopper FREE features basic pop-up and pop-under ad blocking technology. You may be required to hold down the CTRL key to access new links on web pages and email. The Pro and Companion DO NOT have this limitation as they feature a more robust technology.

5

5
The fact that pop-ups can be irritating to the user has led to the rise of numerous pieces of software that remove them from websites. Some adult sites, though, make this nearly impossible as they are desperately trying to get the user to click through. Pop-ups can also be used to carry games. If people want to play but need to surf to another site, the game can stay in the pop-up.

66

HOW ONLINE ADVERTS WORK

When creating an ad campaign that runs across a range of online outlets, you need to understand, at the very least, the principles of what is happening on screen and behind it on the Internet.

Any type of file on the Internet needs to be served from somewhere. In other words, it must be stored on a computer connected to the Internet, with the right software installed for communicating with other computers and sending them the files they request. This type of computer is known both as a server and a host. The files it makes available are said to be hosted on the computer, and served to users.

Third-party hosts

In online advertising, the company carrying the ads is usually responsible for the hosting arrangements, and they will often designate the task to a third-party company. This company should have sophisticated tracking technology for counting how many times each ad is viewed and clicked, where it was seen and by whom, and so on. The key advantage for advertisers is that these should be independent, reliable and undistorted figures—the company stakes its reputation on it, and advertisers and hosts calculate the cost and success of their campaigns relative to the number of visitors and of money-earning clicks.

In some cases, the advertisers themselves prefer to take care of the hosting, particularly where a campaign needs a complex set of technology to work properly—for example, if they plan to tell an evolving storing using cookies at each stage.

At its most basic, putting an ad in a webpage is as simple as adding any other linked image, Flash file or

68

1

2

3

HTML snippet to a page; you simply paste the code in the right place and you're off. If the file is hosted elsewhere, you simply need to provide the full Web address of the file—http://www.somesite.com/ads/imagefile.gif for example.

There are two basic issues for self-hosters, however. First, you'll probably want to use a rotation mechanism, so that ads are not pinned to particular pages and each gets a fair viewing over a particular period of time. Many server applications, such as Microsoft's ASP, have the tools you need built in, or you can download myriad cut-and-paste scripts.

Second, advertisers need a way of seeing which ads on which sites attract the greatest interest; while advertising hosts need a way to count which advertisers' sites visitors are clicking on. A popular way to do this is to provide each ad with a special link, such as redirect.asp?url= http://www.advertiserssite.com/advert.asp?referrer=adcarrier.

Most Web browsers ignore anything that appears after a question mark in a URL, but server technology can use it to perform special actions. In this case, the ad carrier's page redirect.asp will look at the Web address after the question mark—http://www.advertiserssite.com/advert.asp?referrer=adcarrier and send users there instead of displaying the page. It will then make a log entry for future reference. The advertiser's server, meanwhile, will detect the name of the referrer in this redirecting URL, and make its own log entry.

This system demands some special server-side programming, but of course, if you use a company like DoubleClick, it's all taken care of. Here the system may be far more complex, but your third party should simply give you some cut-and-paste code to put in the right place in your webpage HTML. This really is all that's required to get the job done.

69

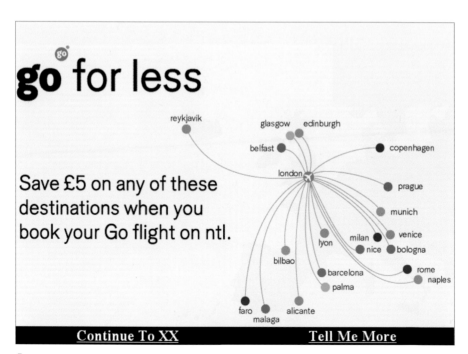

1 | 2 | 3 | 4
Complex ads require more complex technical treatments. Placing interstitials (ads that appear between pages on a site) such as the one here for an airline and creating and linking microsites requires some degree of technical knowledge. Although none of it is actually that complex it can be daunting for someone who hasnt done this before.

ADVERTISING FOR EVERYONE

One major concern relating to placing an advertisement on the Web is how people are going to view it. In the early days of the Web there was real competition between different browsers. For example, Netscape Navigator and Internet Explorer were fairly even competitors. But as time has progressed, Internet Explorer has become dominant and, at best estimates, resides on 85 percent of computers worldwide.

The issue is that, until recently, these browsers interpreted HTML quite differently, and it was difficult to get anything more complex than plain text, an image and a link to work correctly on both without creating two different sets of code.

Things are improving, however, under the auspices of the World Wide Web Consortium (www.w3.org), which has enforced a rigorous set of standards on browser development and coding. The major differences between the browsers from IE version 5 and Netscape version 6 are few, when it comes to the basics at least, and even complex DHTML. But, alas, you can't stop people from using older browsers.

OS variations

There is also the thorny problem of different operating systems, where rendering differences can be quite severe. Apple Macintosh users, for example, still often find that some sites are not designed to work on that operating system, or that elements of it (such as news tickers, for example) malfunction, whereas they work perfectly well with Windows.

In most cases, these problems originate in simple economics. Most users' PCs have Windows as an operating system and most PC users use Internet Explorer as their browser, therefore it is cheaper to design for the majority and accept that some of the audience will be lost. The numbers lost might be relatively small (although the success and popularity

of the iMac is changing that), but they can still be crucial niche audiences. In the case of Mac users in particular, not addressing them can lose you access to large sections of the design, publishing and media industries, as well as to educational markets (students and professors). These sectors use Apple machines extensively. However, by far the majority of the general audience is Windows-based. Your decision, then, is whether or not to pursue these niche audiences, or just aim for the broad home and office-worker market.

Operating system and browser choices can have a severe impact on your decision to deploy DHTML and other more complex technologies.

While the W3C has achieved much in some areas, standards cannot keep pace with technology, and in other areas the situation for designers is getting worse. Palm-tops, email on mobile phones, wireless Internet, interactive TV, Internet-capable games consoles... all of these challenge the accepted formats. At the same time, constant new releases of plug-ins, such as Flash, QuickTime, Real Player, and so on make it impossible to know just what your users do and don't have.

So, the question again is whether to spend money on addressing a niche audience, or to go for the broadest, general one. But, far from being unique to technology, these are the sort of issues advertisers face every day when trying to identify the best medium for a traditional campaign. Despite the new technology, it always comes back to audiences and targeting.

1 | 2 | 3
DHTML ads, such as the "lost in the jungle" one shown here may only work in Microsoft Internet Explorer versions 4 and above, and on Windows only. The ad has to be prepared so that a simple GIF still appears on other browsers, such as Netscape and on MAC OS, but only Windows users will see the animation.

71

GIF ANIMATION

The humble animated GIF has become the staple of Web advertising, with few 468 x 60 banners offering anything different. You just can't beat it for fast-loading, simple, static graphics. Ironically, however, it's not an ideal format for animation: it trades in high file sizes, jagged motion, and lack of control. At the same time, the GIF is the only animated format virtually guaranteed to work on every browser, while the files are comparatively easy to create, which goes some way toward explaining its success.

Today virtually any site will accept animated GIF advertising, although you will certainly be given a maximum file size, and you may be asked to ensure that the ad plays just once without looping. In many cases this has also to be in less than six seconds.

There are myriad applications available for creating GIF animations, from freeware via cheap shareware to fully featured professional suites. The differences between them are in their design capabilities rather than their technical features. Inferior animation applications are rarely bad at creating GIFs, they just don't offer many good creative tools.

However, the rule is that if it works for you, then it works for the Web. All the standard Web graphics packages enable you to create GIF animations, including Photoshop's bundled partner, ImageReady, as well as Fireworks, CorelDraw, and Paint Shop Pro's partner Animation Shop.

The art of creating GIF graphics is to use as few colors as possible: this is what keeps the file size down. When you optimize GIF animations for the Web, you should try to keep the number of colors down to 16, or even just eight, if you possibly can. Fast-loading ads get more clicks.

An animated GIF file is a sequence of static images, or frames. These are also known as layers—but they should not to be confused with the layers that are the core working method of Photoshop and Fireworks.

72

1 | 2 | 3
The Crocodile Hunter animated GIF is effective because the animation reflects what the programme is about. In this case it's a game warden who catches crocodiles by hand.

On each frame you may have a completely different graphic or text; or to create the illusion of motion, you may have a single graphic that changes incrementally. But be aware that your file size escalates with the number of frames you use. Twenty should really be your upper limit in advertising. If allowed, use clever looping to extend the duration of your animation; and carefully set the duration for each frame to get the most out of what it contains.

4 | 5 | 6
The Visa credit card banners are also straightforward animations. The twist here is that they use another high-profile brand, Harley Davidson, to help get the message across. There is also a simple call to action involved in this banner. It asks the user to click.

73

4

5

6

7

7 | 8 | 9
The O_2 banner is simpler, with only the text animating. This is the simplest form of animation.

8

9

FLASH

Flash is a technology developed by Macromedia. It is similar to Shockwave in that it allows advanced animation and functionality to be built and delivered via the Web. All the recent versions of the main browsers have the necessary Flash plug-in already loaded. This ensures that there is no need for anyone to download the plug-in unless they are using a browser older than about five years.

Flash is an authoring package that uses vector-based graphics to reduce file size. Vector graphics are based on simple mathematical principles that define shapes (which can be resized without any loss of quality, unlike bitmaps). Shockwave, on the other hand is based on pixels. These are much larger in file-size terms, so Flash is more preferable for use on the Web.

Because Flash employs vector graphics, the images have a very crisp and clean quality about them. Flash

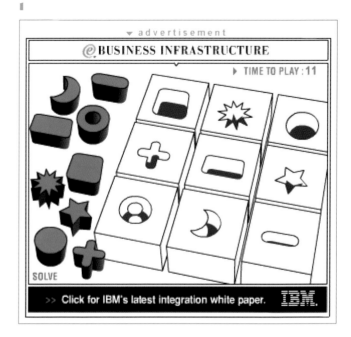

1

2

3

also allows sound to be included via streaming technology and it makes audio in banner advertisements a real possibility.

Flash banners can be designed to take full advantage of the available functionality. Many Flash banners contain active data entry boxes, and they can include expanding windows that increase the size of the ad. For instance, many advertisers make use of the functionality to allow users to expand a banner and read a list. With Flash a long menu can roll out from the banner and also allow a user to engage in commerce via the banner directly with no need to visit another site.

In a lot of ways this answers many criticisms levelled at Web advertising. The file sizes are small, the functionality is advanced. The ad can give an immersive experience, yet leave the user on their original site.

In addition, scripting in Flash has also become much more sophisticated. In its early incarnations, Flash had only a limited authoring or scripting language thereby restricting the software's creativity, but later versions have seen the expansion of what is called Action Script. This powerful scripting language has brought Flash to a point where in some ways it can compete with Director's Lingo. Action Script means that real and very accurate control can be hard-coded into an ad and that a Flash movie can be fast and highly interactive.

Flash provides high-impact, clean-looking ads that can be real head turners in themselves.

1 | 2 | 3 | 4 | 5

In this example, Flash has been used to create a game that is clean, effective, and quick to launch and play. Flash gives the clean lines and flat colors that are used to such good effect here.

4

5

JAVASCRIPT, CSS, AND DHTML

HTML is a language for displaying information and linking to files—it can't actually "do" anything. When Web designers want a webpage to make a calculation, or perform a bit of logic, they usually use JavaScript embedded in the HTML. JavaScript could be used for changing an image as part of a rollover, dynamically adjusting the contents of a form field, or opening a pop-up window. The code looks daunting, but it's relatively simple. Moreover, it can only access things in webpages, it can't access your computer in any way.

Cascading Style Sheets is another simple language used in HTML to control the positioning and appearance of elements. A simple CSS rule, like img { border: 1px solid red } tells a CSS compliant browser to put a one-pixel solid red border around all images.

Dynamic HTML

DHTML, in which the D stands for "dynamic," is simply a hybrid of JavaScript, CSS, and HTML that creates fast-loading designs that can move, change, interact, and process information.

If you have ever seen an ad fly across a page or a graphic following your mouse around, then it's probably been done in DHTML. DHTML is powerful when used well but annoying when deployed indisriminately. Indeed, DHTML ad designers have fallen into the habit of using guerrilla tactics to attract more clicks. This can do more harm than good: if every time a user logs onto a search engine and finds half the page obscured by moving objects, then they will cease to visit the site.

But used sparingly, DHTML is an effective weapon in your armory. A winter promotion might be greatly enhanced by the addition of snowflakes falling down the page. A motor-racing promotion can be made more inviting if, as the page is loaded, cars screech and race across the page. If nothing else, it will hold the visitor's attention the first time they visit. The most creative uses

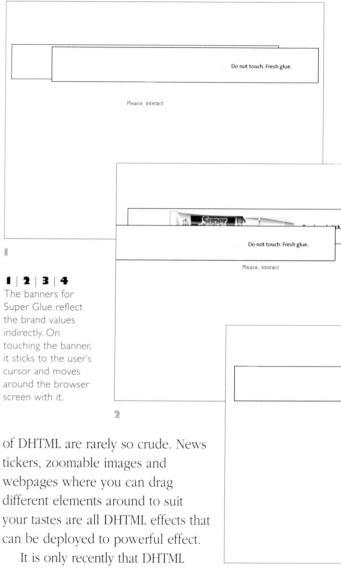

1 | 2 | 3 | 4
The banners for Super Glue reflect the brand values indirectly. On touching the banner, it sticks to the user's cursor and moves around the browser screen with it.

of DHTML are rarely so crude. News tickers, zoomable images and webpages where you can drag different elements around to suit your tastes are all DHTML effects that can be deployed to powerful effect.

It is only recently that DHTML standards have been thrashed out and taken up by the major browsers (version 5 and up), which is why we are seeing a great increase in DHTML ads. Previously, getting anything with much impact to work on all browser/platform combinations was nigh-on impossible. This is still true today if you need to cater for users with older software. Be warned!

5

5
The moving "robot arm" shows DHTML techniques to great effect. Linked to a banner for microprocessors, this is an effective brand message tie-up.

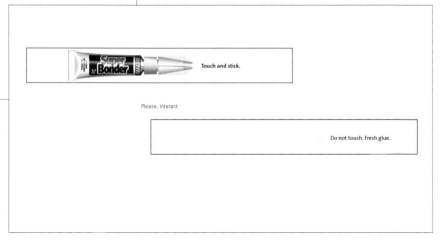

The key to many DHTML ads is a feature variously known as layers, DIVs, and "absolutely positioned block-level elements." But we're probably better off thinking of them as floating boxes. They can be styled and positioned anywhere on a page using JavaScript and/or CSS, and float over other content. The box itself is usually denoted with a <div> tag, and its content is ordinary HTML.

Learning to write DHTML is quite an undertaking, although it is nothing to be scared of. Most Web-authoring apps, like Dreamweaver and GoLive, come with reams of automated DHTML options that enable you to choose the actions you want to occur, and when, and nothing more. There are also several excellent free cut-and-paste DHTML/JavaScript resources on the Internet—try www.javascript.com and www.dynamicdrive.com for starters.

JAVA

Java, despite its name, has nothing to do with JavaScript; in fact it is a completely different language. Java is an out and out "true" programming language, requiring a good level of programming skill in order to extract the most from it. Most coding carried out tends to be undertaken in what are called authoring environments. Authoring languages, which are closer to everyday language, act as a sort of interface between the "programmer" and the coding that the computer understands. Java is a programming language; JavaScript is a scripting or authoring language.

The most common Java programs are either complete applications or smaller applications known as applets. While applications are standalone programs, applets are similar to them, but they don't run by themselves. Instead, they adhere to a set of conventions that lets them run within a Java-compatible browser.

Java, because it is so powerful, allows highly interactive banners and content to be produced. The banners can have changing text, changing colors, wipe effects, high levels of interactivity, music and sound, scrolling text and much more. Java is highly efficient in terms of keeping file size small, thereby improving download times. It

78

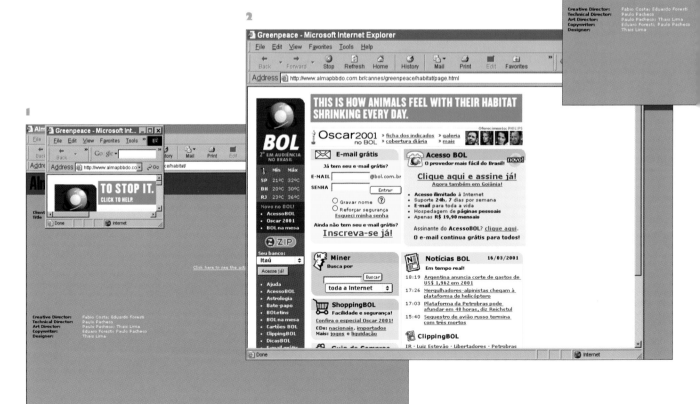

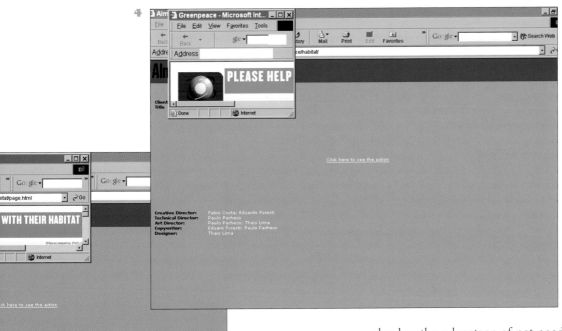

4 Alm... Greenpeace - Microsoft Int...
File | File Edit View Favorites Tools
Back | Back | gle |
Addre | Address | ce/habitat/

Alm... PLEASE HELP
Client
Title
Done | Internet

Click here to see the action

Creative Director: Fabio Costa; Eduardo Foresti
Technical Director: Paulo Pacheco
Art Director: Paulo Pacheco; Thais Lima
Copywriter: Eduaro Foresti; Paulo Pacheco
Designer: Thais Lima

Google | Google |
abitat/page.html | Go
L WITH THEIR HABITAT
Oferecimento: PRU...
Internet
Click here to see the action

1 | 2 | 3 | 4
In these Greenpeace ads, the power of hard coding banners can be seen. The ad message is simple— natural habitats are shrinking. The users' window shrinks in the same way while the message in the banner changes to fit the changing window size. The technology is used to directly illustrate the message in an unexpected way.

5 | 6 | 7 | 8
The sample Java banners containing the quiz also demonstrate the power of coding banners and creating real interactivity. People love quizzes—the banners tap into that.

Pick the correct big word that matches the definition. (big words)

5

erucation | discombobulation | suppuration
2. The act of belching   0/4 (big words)

6

3. To throw from a window.   2/4 (big words)
pontificate | matriculate | defenestrate

7

3. To throw (big words)
pontificate

8

also has the advantage of not needing plug-ins or downloaded players, as is the case with Shockwave and Flash.

Java banners can be used to deliver small, fun games and content to users in ways that other formats cannot. They offer the greatest degree of control of all the formats discussed here. With Java a banner can become a full, small application. Users can be given paint brushes or be asked to scratch to remove a layer, and they can also do highly interesting things such as using pointers to project missiles (throw something). Because Java is a programming language, its level of sophistication ensures that absolute fine control can be gained.

The big disadvantage is that many surfers have historically turned off Java in their browser options to speed up their surfing. However, this is increasingly less of a problem, particularly on sites aimed at the general user.

In considering using Java, the same old rules apply. Look at what is required from the ad and where it will go for audience reasons and then make the decision as to which way to proceed.

SHOCKWAVE

Shockwave is proprietary software developed by Macromedia. Files from Director, a multimedia authoring tool produced by Macromedia, can be saved in Shockwave format, allowing them to be delivered via the Web. Director makes it easy to include video and audio in interactive ways not possible with HTML.

When a Shockwave application is created, it is compressed into a format that makes it smaller in file size, thereby reducing the time it takes to download. It is still not advisable to produce anything large but files of 200KB are not uncommon. Compared with a banner of 12KB, this is a big move forward.

Shockwave movies do still have to be small though, and usually they are delivered in a format that has a small active area. So a typical game might be 200 x 300 pixels. This helps keep memory down. It is also necessary to restrict the size because a shockwave movie cannot be resized by the browser.

1

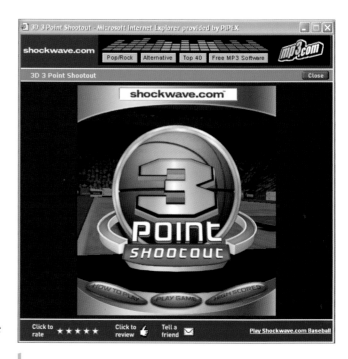

2

3

4

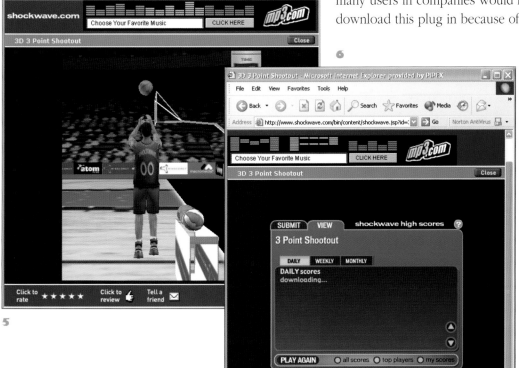

5

The real strength of Shockwave is that its parent program, Director, allows for complex coding, which means it is easy to create games in this format. It has become so popular for this purpose that Macromedia themselves support an extensive gallery of games produced by users, found at www.shockwave.com.

Shockwave is a very powerful tool for creating interactive games carrying low overheads. They can offer limited 3D graphics, be multiplayer (at a cost for extra multi user licenses), give support to fully interactive leader boards, and be used for data collection.

The attraction for advertisers becomes obvious. Media and graphically rich, highly interactive experiences that can add real value to a campaign can be cheaply produced in this format.

The drawbacks come through the need to keep things small for download and the fact that users need to download a plug in. Unlike Flash, Macromedia's other interactive media product, the plug in, is not necessarily installed in the user's browser. It is worth noting that many users in companies would not be able to download this plug in because of company firewalls.

81

6

1 | 2 | 3 | 4 | 5 | 6
This game created in Shockwave clearly illustrates the power of the medium. The game is in pseudo 3D and replicates the experience of throwing a basketball at a hoop. It is also capable of linking up to high score tables so that the user can compete against everyone using it. Shockwave games as ads are quite rare because of the application's technical limitations. However, in the correct context they can be very powerful.

DYNAMIC CONTENT

It has long been a feature of websites to place ticker tapes in browser control bars, but the move to placing similar feeds in banners is an intriguing one.

Dynamic updateable content is exactly analogous to this. A user can view an ad and know that the information within it is literally up to the minute.

There are technologies being used that allow for dynamic updating. Using Java, information can be uploaded live to banners, pop-ups and other formats. The main reason for pursuing this route is to make sure that users get first sight of the latest product news. The same technology can be used to plug into databases. This is important because it means that a user can request up-to-date information. Timetables, prices, and news are just three forms of content that would benefit from dynamic updating.

Improved efficiency

Such technology ensures that a marketing department can update content without having to go back to an agency to make costly changes.

Many sites have yet to agree to carry ads like this as they feel that the technology is still not fully proven and, as with all new methods, advertisers have also been somewhat nervous.

As with many other developments, however, it seems that active real-time updateable ads will play an increasing part in online advertising. As systems get smarter, and as advertisers learn to tell exactly who is looking at their ads, they will naturally want to feed them targeted, accurate information and content.

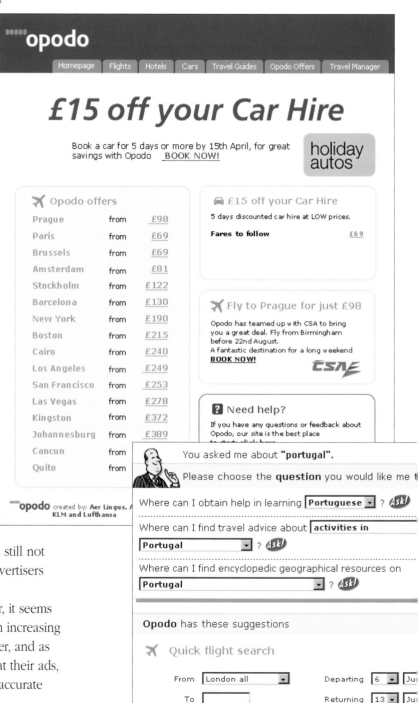

3

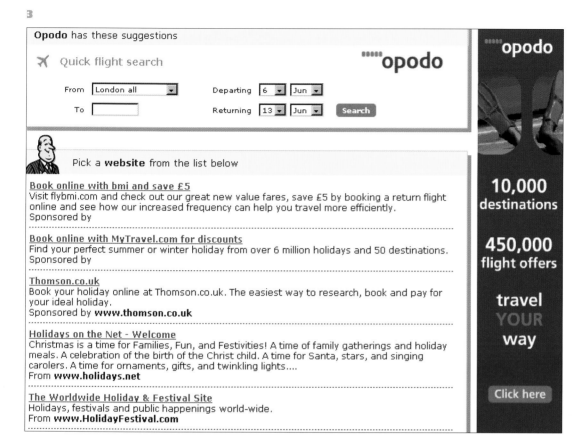

Opodo has these suggestions

✈ Quick flight search

""""opodo

From [London all ▼]   Departing [6 ▼] [Jun ▼]
To [_____]   Returning [13 ▼] [Jun ▼]   [Search]

Pick a **website** from the list below

Book online with bmi and save £5
Visit flybmi.com and check out our great new value fares, save £5 by booking a return flight online and see how our increased frequency can help you travel more efficiently.
Sponsored by

Book online with MyTravel.com for discounts
Find your perfect summer or winter holiday from over 6 million holidays and 50 destinations.
Sponsored by

Thomson.co.uk
Book your holiday online at Thomson.co.uk. The easiest way to research, book and pay for your ideal holiday.
Sponsored by **www.thomson.co.uk**

Holidays on the Net - Welcome
Christmas is a time for Families, Fun, and Festivities! A time of family gatherings and holiday meals. A celebration of the birth of the Christ child. A time for Santa, stars, and singing carolers. A time for ornaments, gifts, and twinkling lights....
From **www.holidays.net**

The Worldwide Holiday & Festival Site
Holidays, festivals and public happenings world-wide.
From **www.HolidayFestival.com**

opodo

10,000
destinations

450,000
flight offers

travel
YOUR
way

[Click here]

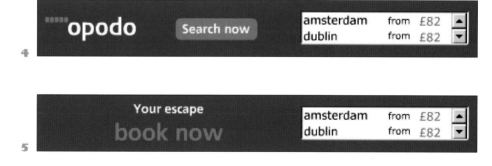

4

opodo [Search now]   amsterdam from £82 ▲
dublin from £82 ▼

5

Your escape
book now   amsterdam from £82 ▲
dublin from £82 ▼

1 | 2 | 3 | 4 | 5

In the examples here for Opodo, a cheap flights search and brokering service, the nature of the brand matches the dynamic execution. Most people looking for air fares online want accurate information from databases. They also want to know what the latest prices are for flights. Dynamic real time updateable ads can access the flights' database and allow users to search, or roll the latest offers across the banner as the user does something else, such as browsing an entertainment or news site.

SMS, WAP, IMODE, ITV

The most recent digital formats have seen advertising spread across into other digital media. New forms have appeared and have immediately been exploited for advertising purposes.

Short Message Service (SMS) on mobile phones has exploded in use. There are literally billions of SMS messages sent every week. Imaging is virtually non-existent at present, and the presentation is monochrome—but that will change in time as more and more mobile phones use color LCD displays. However, the impact of SMS is massive because the message arrives in the user's hand directly, and with efficient targeting can be extremely effective. In the main mobile phone territories, advertising has become a major industry on SMS services.

WAP and iMode

These are systems that allow the user to explore what are essentially mini websites. They can be used to find out information, such as the latest news headlines, sports results, and financial news, or on a less serious note, play games on. They have the basic functionality of most Web services. Users can request information, send information, and engage in dialog with an advertiser, albeit in a rather slow inefficient way.

Many campaigns on mobile phones use external triggers to drive consumers to them. Chocolate bar wrappers might, for instance, carry numbers for a user to text in if they want to win a prize. Similarly, with more active data services, campaigns usually use offline media to kickstart them.

84

1 – 8

The illustrations here show screen grabs from a range of interactive TV ads and from WAP and SMS campaigns. Technical issues limit their functionality. On mobile media, screens tend to be mono-chromatic (though that is changing) and not very large. On TV the resolution is also low and functionality limited by the interactive TV technology.

9 – 16

All these examples have one thing in common with most Web ads. They all possess a call to action and all record users clicks.

The main advantages of these media seem to be that they are highly personal, can be targeted at individuals and, with the click of one button, the user can reply. An added advantage is of course that the consumer pays for the messages themselves.

Interactive TV is also appearing on the horizon as a medium to watch. The most developed market for this is in the UK where by 2003, 40 percent of the population had gone over to digital TV systems, which offer interactivity. Often these systems work similarly to the Web in that an iTV ad can take the viewer to a microsite. The difference here is that often the call to action is a trigger from a TV commercial. A symbol appears and with one click the user jumps into the interactive version of the ad.

Although iTV has certain similarities with the Web, it also differs in that the people who use it are watching TV, not surfing the Web. This means that their behavior is fundamentally different.

All these media have appeared in a very short space of time and have served to confuse an already opaque digital advertising scene even further. Again, however, in the right context they can be incredibly effective.

9

10

11

12

13

14

15

16

PROPOSITION

All products and services need marketing or advertising. In every field of commerce, there are always new entrants to a particular market that offer either new deals, or better prices, and so on. The use of well-executed advertising and marketing helps to maintain the position of a company or service within its marketplace.

With traditional media such as newspapers or TV, the planning process behind making and placing ads is relatively straightforward. In simple terms, the company allocates a budget after which a decision is taken on how best to use the budget to maximum effect.

Traditional media are inherently narrow in terms of their audience. Publications are already targeted toward certain audiences, as are TV and radio channels and programs. The decision process can make good use of this information in order to find the most cost-effective route to the correct group of consumers.

Web for all

The Web, on the other hand, has grown up in a haphazard and individual way. Lack of regulation and ease of access to the network has meant that instead of corporations owning the rights to broadcast and carry content, individuals have been able to do so, and to compete with the big players.

As the Web matures, we are seeing a slow change in that major corporations are moving in and consolidating their presence. However, the Web is still the one medium where an individual can get access to the same reach as a corporation. Many top sites were ones started by individuals, Yahoo being a case in point, and aintitcoolnews being another.

The Web is also unique in that enthusiasts, fans, and interested parties can set up their own presence in a way that is much easier and that has much greater reach than traditional media can offer.

1
The rise of the fansite and unofficial celebratory sites, such as Stars Wars Bloopers, has given advertisers a way of targeting specific groups of people. The ad on this page is for courses related to filmmaking which is a good fit with the brand.

This means that a company choosing to advertise on the Web will have a more difficult time deciding where to place ads and in what format to present them to maximize their reach and impact.

Research, of course, is everything. Knowing your audience has never been so important, and knowing your proposition even more so. In other words, knowing what you want to say and to whom is vital. Advertisers have to understand whether their proposition is best advertised across fan or enthusiast sites, or via large corporate sites or service portals such as AOL. It may be that the ads are best delivered in a game format within a related interest site, or it may be that a microsite and unique domain might be more effective.

89

2 | 3
Big companies place ads on fansites to maximize impact. The two examples here show ads for books, DVDs, CDs and so on in the context of a list of fansites about movies and TV.

WHAT OPPORTUNITIES ARE AVAILABLE?

Logging onto Google.com, the user is confronted with a stark fact, namely the number of pages that have been counted by that search engine through its various mechanisms. This number is in billions and steadily rising by the day.

In terms of the number of actual sites, we may never know how many there are out there, or how many individuals are accessing them (many people use multiple log-ons). Some sites are very popular and attract huge numbers of viewers, while others are virtually abandoned like cyber ghost towns gathering virtual dust.

Clearly, it is in the interest of large sites and portals to track user information and statistics very closely. In terms of raising advertising revenue, sites must be able to provide accurate figures, as these form the advertising proposition to interested parties.

It is no good placing ads on sites that have few viewers, or large numbers of visitors who fall outside the target audience. Even when using banner exchange schemes, where individuals allow banners to appear on their sites in return for free access to certain services, an advertiser cannot be guaranteed the reach they need.

1 | 2 | 3
A simple look at Sony's worldwide sites shows that it localizes its presence, and each territory has a different look and feel. Online advertising has to show the same sensitivity to local conditions.

In the case of an exchange scheme, the advertiser can never be sure that anyone will visit the sites on which the ads are placed. This is why the larger advertisers have started to use the more "corporate" outlets for advertising.

Internationally, the number of sites maintained by large companies is growing. Each main Internet territory has its own Yahoo! site, for example. Most large companies, such as Sony, have local or regional sites. Internet service providers (ISPs) also have their own local portals. AOL has portals in all the major territories, and Amazon is recognizably Amazon whatever the language.

91

Cross advertising

AOL, Disney, and other "family" sites are obvious targets for ad placement across territories. It is a relatively simple decision to use these sites as they invariably have the same audiences and the same appeal in whatever country they are being served from. AOL is a family portal; Disney is a children and family brand. Advertising family products across sites such as these guarantees access to a family audience.

Sports, however, have no such common, global sites. Sports fans in the USA and the UK, in Japan and Australia, all have different tastes. It is no good anticipating a worldwide reach on a site dedicated to the baseball World Series when in Europe virtually no one is interested. In Europe the bigger sports portals tend to use soccer as their main sport. Advertising via the World Series might attain good reach in the USA and Japan, but soccer would be the obvious channel in the UK and Germany, for example.

There are very few large brands whose reach is truly international in the way that Disney's and Coca-Cola's is. This means that, like traditional media, the online ad campaign has to be developed with local audiences in mind, a point that contradicts the very notion of the Web as a worldwide medium.

SO WHO IS OUT THERE?

The number of Internet users is the subject of much debate. Over the next pages we will examine the current estimates, look more closely at the most popular sites and identify trends. The sheer scale of the Web makes it ever more crucial to understand where the real opportunities lie.

Nua Internet Surveys (www.nua.net) estimated that as of February 2002 there were 544.2 million Internet users—a $\frac{1}{12}$th of the world's population. It is clear that newspapers, TV and radio have greater penetration but none have achieved it at this rate of growth. Overall this spectacular rise seems unlikely to stop. The same Nua survey also shows the breakdown by region: Africa 4.15 million, Asia/Pacific 157.49 million, Europe 171.35 million, Middle East 4.65 million, Canada & USA 181.23 million, and Latin America 25.33 million.

Website numbers

As of January 2002, it was estimated by the Internet Software Consortium (http://www.isc.org) that there were 147,344,723 separate websites as counted by hosts. This is far from a conclusive list. It also shows that the growth from January 1993 was spectacular. At this time, the figure quoted was 1,313,000. This means that in just nine years over 146 million new websites appeared.

There are more non-native English speakers on the Web than there are native ones. According to Nua surveys, "around 59.8 percent of the total world online population are from non-English speaking zones, compared to 40.2 percent from English speaking zones. This is equivalent to 338.5 million non-English Internet users and 22.8 million English speaking users."

Nielsen Net Ratings (http://www.nielsen-netratings.com) continually survey Internet usage and, in terms of how much people use the Web, a quick glance at its latest survey results reveals that the Web is rapidly becoming a mainstream medium.

MARCH 2002 GLOBAL INTERNET INDEX AVERAGE USAGE*

	March	February
Number of Sessions per Month	19	17
Number of Unique Domains Visited	47	44
Page Views per Month	826	773
Page Views per Surfing Session	43	45
Time Spent per Month	10:14:17	9:35:5
Time Spent During Surfing Session	0:32:13	0:33:13
Duration of a Page Viewed	0:00:45	0:00:45

*Home Internet Access

All of the statistics above demonstrate the necessity to drill down and really understand your audience.

2

Le Monde.fr screenshot (Le Monde.fr website, lundi 27 mai 2002, "La violence sur les écrans de télévision")

Around the world people are going online and most sites carry localized advertising which belies the perception in the West that English is the *lingua Franca* of the Web.

93

3

City of Life — Hong Kong is it! website screenshot

"Life is an event. Hong Kong is a non-stop celebration. HSBC Mega Hong Kong Sale"

Hi,
From now until March 2003, you are invited to participate in a festive celebration of our lifestyle, culture and traditions. A fusion of East and West in the City of Life.

Hong Kong This Week
An upbeat musical, a popular Japanese violinist and the best of Italian culture in the city where East meets West >>

Headline News
• Quaint villages set amongst breathtaking scenery await visitors to Tai Po District >>

MEASURING

As we have discussed, sites that take advertising as part of their business plan will always track usage carefully. Sites such as Yahoo! and MSN know what pages are viewed, how long a user stays on the site, how many times they visit over any given period, what they link to, and, where possible, they will know who the user is. This is vital for an advertiser to know because a campaign will be based on these figures.

Counting impressions

So what are the main measures of usage? The first term we hear about is "page impression." This often misunderstood term simply refers to the number of times a specific webpage has been accessed or viewed by a user. As such, it is not a reliable guide for advertisers, as it does not identify how many unique users visit a site. In other words, a page impression merely acts as a counter. Page impressions are also referred to as "hits."

By contrast, unique users are measured according to their unique IP addresses. Unique visitors are counted only once no matter how many times they visit the site, and this is therefore a much more reliable indicator of customer numbers.

One other term that we need to look out for is "impression." An impression is simply the number of times an ad appears on a webpage. Advertisers use impressions to measure the number of views their ads receive, and publishers often sell ad space according to this metric. This is not really an accurate measure of success, as viewers might switch off graphics, or might never scroll down far enough to see the ad.

It might sound unappealing, but it is equally important to measure failures. Pages on the host's site that fail to load are a waste of the advertiser's money. This does happen, so there is a need to check.

To get a more accurate measure, MSN has adopted a system called Passport. This provides a user with a single log-in for all MSN and other participating services. The payback for Microsoft is that the user has to surrender a level of personal information. This information means that MSN knows, with a fair degree of accuracy, who its users are. This is not a sinister "big brother" style development, rather a way for the portal to be able to do two things. One, sell advertising more effectively, and two, make the content of the site more responsive to its audience.

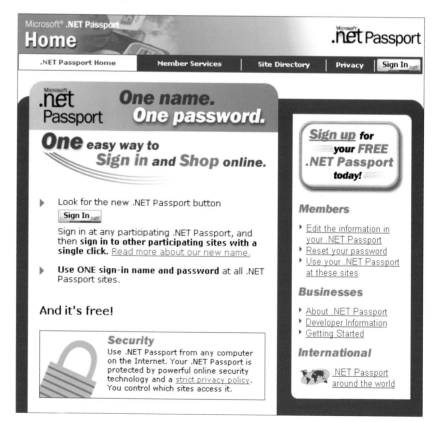

2

Microsoft® .NET Passport

Member Services

Registration

Completing this form will register you with .NET Passport Web Site and with Microsoft® .NET Passport. With .NET Passport, you can use the e-mail address and password you provide below to sign in to any site that has the .NET Passport sign-in button.

| Sign In net | Click the .NET Passport sign-in button if you have already registered for a .NET Passport at another site. (All @hotmail.com and @msn.com e-mail addresses are .NET Passports.) |

Fields marked with ⬈ will be stored in your .NET Passport.   **Help**

E-mail Address   email@emailaccount.net   ⬈

Password   ••••••••   ⬈
Six-character minimum; no spaces

Retype Password   ⬈

Tired of registration forms? You can speed reg personalized services at participating sites by sh Passport information with them when you sign in boxes below to choose how much of your .NET F information Microsoft can share with other compa Passport sites at sign-in:

☐ Share my e-mail address.

Tell me more about .NET Passport, privacy, and

1 | 2 | 3
The MSN passport system is very simple to set up and is the clearest illustration yet of the way firms are moving toward more accurate measures of traffic by personally profiling each user. This is a radical step away from the general demographic measurements usually adopted by traditional media. Where traditional and digital are linked, of course (in the case of magazine websites that add value to their printed counterparts), a company can gather a great deal of information about their "traditional" customers as well.

95

Microsoft® .NET Passport

Member Services

Registration Is Complete

Thank you for registering the following e-mail address as your Microsoft® .NET Passport:

email@emailaccount.net

Remember:
Sign in with your .NET Passport e-mail address and password wherever you see the .NET Passport sign-in button.

To make online shopping fast, easy, and more secure:
Click here to create your .NET Passport wallet now

Continue

Microsoft®
.net

Member Services   Terms of Use   Privacy Statement

Microsoft.net

Any site that participates in Microsoft's .net Passport has been vetted by Microsoft and is, therefore, likely to be secure and genuine.

MSN and similar portals have to maintain and develop their services, and consequently rely on advertising to help cover the considerable expense. Without accurate figures, advertisers are unlikely to buy ad space on these sites.

3

MORE ABOUT WHO IS OUT THERE

A lot of the information that is gathered about who is on the Web is, by nature, concentrated in the biggest online markets. The sheer scale of the US and European markets tends to obscure what is going on elsewhere in terms of usage. If a large brand decides to advertise worldwide on the Web, it has to look further than its own back yard. For instance, in South Africa, recent surveys quoted at www.nua.com/surveys discovered that the word "jobs" has overtaken "sex" as the most popular search term. Other popular words used for searching, according to the report were "lotto," "SMS," "maps," "property," and "cricket." Further research on Nua points to the fact that nearly 60 percent of the total world online population is in non-English speaking zones. Global brands, therefore, have to think outside English as their main Web language.

A few brands have set up Chinese operations—a number of high-tech firms and other large corporations operate from there as well as from other parts of the world. Of course, many of these sites never appear in search engines, as the necessary character set is absent. But it is always worth attempting a Web search in a foreign language, such as French, German, or Spanish. It doesn't occur to many English-speaking people to do this, but a quick search in any European language will rapidly persuade of the untapped audience out there.

1

2

3

1
News sites will help you to find out who is on the Web. Online news services tend to pick up the headline figures which when aggregated provide good sources of information.

2 | 3
Major sites all have versions in other languages. These tend to use the same design, reflecting the fact that online brands can become truly international with little difficulty.

Global growth

Netsense (http://www.netsenseindia.com/) in India, monitors Internet usage there. The researchers have found that by mid-2002 over 48 percent of schoolchildren in India were accessing the Internet at cybercafes.

Netsense also highlights some similarities with Web users around the world: Yahoo! is the "stickiest" site among schoolchildren, accounting for 61.3 percent of visitors (in 2002 research), while Hotmail, India Times, and MSN account for 23.1 percent, 17.5 percent, and 14.4 percent, respectively.

It is apparent from these figures that some sites have compelling propositions outside of their traditional territories. MSN, Yahoo!, and Hotmail appear in top ten domain lists around the world (although, as many Hotmail users know, they get redirected automatically to MSN when they log out of their email accounts).

In China, in May 2002, the official figures for Web access stood at 37.5 million, which out of a population of over 1 billion sounds like a small number, but it is the equivalent of well over half of the total UK population. Bear in mind that telephone penetration is relatively low in China, so the percentage of people with a telephone who also surf the Web is relatively high.

The Web is no longer Western centric. Increasingly, markets are opening up in other territories outside the "early adopter" countries. This makes it increasingly important to begin targeting ad campaigns more accurately. Ads can be served in multiple languages using software that knows where the receiving computer is. So, in terms of targeting, advertisers need to get smart.

5

4

4 | 5
News sites are among those that have versions of their offerings in a number of languages. These can provide the advertiser with an easy way to reach a very wide audience. However, adverts that appear on multilingual sites have to be created with due sensitivity to a great variety of local cultures.

SOCIAL AND MARKET RESEARCH

If we are to know how to target an intended audience then it is necessary to know what they are doing online. Different audience segments frequently have the capacity to surprise advertisers by behaving contrary to people's expectations.

For example, one of the largest groups of Web users in the UK are the so-called "silver surfers" (people of late middle age and older) who use the Web for banking and share trading. In fact it is this age group that has been the main users of one of the new breed of online-only banks (www.egg.com), which means that they have readily accepted new brands (even ones that appear to have been designed for a much younger audience.)

This flies in the face of conventional advertising wisdom that paints over 55s as being slow to accept new products, and it demonstrates that in the online world, success is more than ever down to service.

2

1

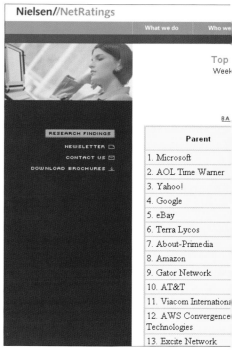

3

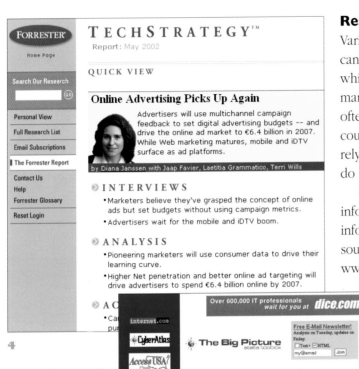

Research on the Web

Various companies engage in research. Any ad agency can point toward the numerous research sources from which they develop their planning. There are, however, many sources that are available free and online. There is often no guarantee that online research is accurate, of course (there is no "badge" of quality on the Web!), and relying on one source would be foolish. However, trends do emerge from a scan of free surveys.

Online newspapers are also good sources of information. Journalists will have access to verified information and, therefore, are among the more trusted sources. http://www.spiegel.de/, http://www.lemonde.fr, www.guardian.co.uk, www.wsj.com, and www.ft.com are all trusted online newspaper sites for research. There are, of course, many, many more.

There are also sites that do the job of aggregating research and representing it in a way that allows users to find things easily. In the ad research field, Nua (www.nua.net) is a good port of call, as is Cyberatlas at http://cyberatlas.internet.com.

Major research companies all have online presences too. Jupiter MMXI, Nielsen NetRating and many others allow free access to a limited set of statistics, which are enough to give a flavor of what is happening. However, it can be easier to buy the relevant report from their selections.

Many larger brands have even started to employ social anthropologists. These are people who are trained to study behavior, and behavioral understanding is becoming key to successful online ad campaigns. Finding out who the audience is, where they are and what they are likely to be doing when they receive the ad are central to an online campaign's success.

1
www.egg.com is a UK-based online bank whose initial branding was as "something new." However, it has become a favorite of older customers, which flies in the face of conventional wisdom.

2 | 3 | 4 | 5
There are many research companies offering varying levels of service. The free sites, such as NUA, can be illuminating as they often aggregate findings from major reports by the larger research companies, such as Forrester, Nielsen, and Jupiter MMXI.

99

TARGETING

Finding out what the audience is doing when they receive an ad online is crucial to its success. This means that targeting is becoming increasingly important.

Targeting tools are becoming very sophisticated and ad serving and management companies such as doubleClick can target ads even down to the level of individual IP addresses.

So, when creating a campaign, it's of vital importance to know who the user is. Being able to target down to individual IP addresses means that two people sitting next to each other in the same building and on the same network could receive different ads in different languages, but selling them the same product.

For example, imagine that one of the two users is Dutch and one is French but both are studying at a university in London. They might be looking at a Dutch site and at a French site, but their IP address will identify where they are. An advertiser trying to reach these students could deliver ads in French and Dutch, selling the same product from London.

Less complex and controversial ways of targeting are based on what the audience is viewing. Recently some advertisers have begun to use session-based targeting. That is, they have bought up most of the ad space on a site and delivered a "story" as the user progresses through the site, with various calls to action built in along the way. This approach may well prove to be profitable, but to be truly effective it does rely on the advertiser knowing who views the site.

Other ways of targeting are to use keywords on search engines or by implementing affiliate or banner exchange schemes where users display banners on their sites in return for an incentive. This means that small sites that are part of larger common interest groups can be used to reach individuals.

When preparing a campaign it is normal to consider all the alternatives for targeting. Ad agencies will always explore whether a particular method is right for the product being advertised.

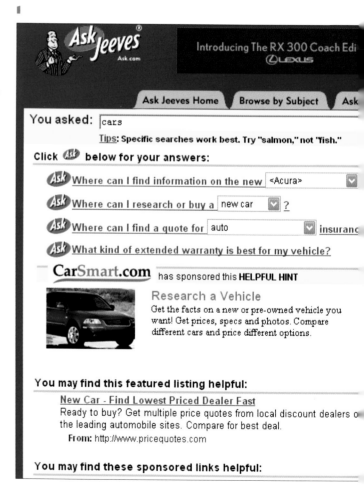

On Ask.com, sometimes banners are served based on words in the user search and sometimes users are directed to sponsored links. Targeted ads delivered in this way can be very effective.

2 | 3 | 4

On Google, targeted ads, based on user requests, appear as simple links either above or beside the search results.

2

3

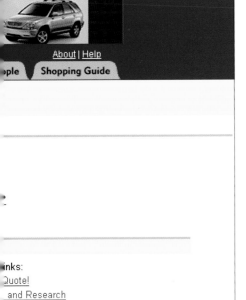

About | Help

Shopping Guide

inks:
Quote!
and Research
re & Compare
Reviews

ar fast. Submit simple, no-obligation forms powered by

LET OTHERS DO THE WORK!

There are many ways that online advertising campaigns can be organized. One, of course, is to take a similar approach to television advertising. Identify two or three key sites, buy space, and then advertise on them. However, this approach is becoming increasingly expensive and there's no guarantee that you'll always catch the right audience.

Various other models have appeared that operate in different ways. Two key strategies are affiliate marketing and banner exchange schemes. Both of these can get an advert directly to interested parties without the expense of a broad brush "big hit" approach.

Affiliate and banner exchange

Affiliate schemes operate on a simple principle. Companies place ads on their sites in return for a share of revenue from any customers that are driven there from that advert. So, if an ad for football videos is placed on a site and lots of people visit the seller's site from that ad, then the ad hosting site will receive a commission. This means that banner placement costs are reduced.

Affiliate schemes require an advertiser to know exactly what their proposition is, who it appeals to, and where the best sites are. Without this intelligence the system will be ineffective.

Banner exchange schemes are a slight variant of this, but, again, are very popular with special interest networks. A banner exchange is a free service designed to help advertise and promote a website. By inserting a small piece of code (usually supplied by the exchange organizers) on a webpage, that page will display banner advertisements from other exchange members. In return, your banner will be displayed across the exchange network. This is also usually charged by the click. If it generates traffic then the exchange scheme organizer takes commission.

1
The IBM affiliate banner scheme allows member sites to use IBM banner advertisements on their sites in return for commission if anyone clicks through to IBM from them. In many cases IBM even supplies ready-made banner adverts, as is shown in the example here.

2
ClickZ is a site that exists through the contributions of its own communities. Such sites are targets for advertisers as the audience is known.

| Home | Products & services | Support & do |

888-SHOP-IBM

Gain access to the best merchandising in the

- Market IBM products with the best banners, p product showcases (storefronts).

IBM. **In the parallel universe, data difficult to use.**

- "Hot Deals" that will optimize your site's click

IBM. **Hot D**

- Or, allow IBM to do all of the work. Automatic your site through Auto-Merchandiser.

with your
online
purchase
of any

Hit refresh to see some of

See Auto-Merchandiser in actio
Electronic Busines
CDML Computer S

2

103

uter industry

t shots, search boxes

nd sales.

s

tate time sensitive offers on

rrent offers.

ome affiliate sites:
ems
, Ltd.

The pursuit of evermore effective ways of advertising to specifically targeted groups has seen the emergence of supported specialist websites. Companies with specialist as opposed to mass-market advertising needs, such as electronics or plumbing suppliers, have begun to see the value of supporting specialist interest sites related to their products. In other words, they accept sponsorship—an old technique, but a very effective one that is being increasingly used on the Web. ClickZ.com, one of the foremost online advertising journals, is a good example of a site that does this.

EMAIL ADVERTISING

As targeting has become more sophisticated and the audience on the Web has grown and diversified away from the "computer worker" base, many different ways of advertising have emerged. Affiliate and exchange systems have been successful, but one of the most effective tools for advertisers has turned out to be one of the simplest—email, the original "killer app" of the Internet.

Email advertising makes use of the fact that everyone on the Web is likely to use email regularly, so an advertisement dropping into the user's inbox is an obvious way to reach them.

In the early days this was exciting, and news of new sites and the latest products was helpful to receive. After a while, though, the number of emails became overwhelming and a new term entered the lexicon of users, "spamming." This is the delivering of unsolicited emails and it is the single most annoying thing on the Internet.

NEW! **Ep II Actic Geonosis** The Battle the Geono Droids, clc survival. This next Action Figure Background p recreate this exciting scene with your favorite E "suggested action figures" to see a list of toys display with this background. Oh, and make st Click here to view and print now.

NEW! **Getting Into Ep II: Heroes & Villains, Part II** In Episode I, we learned that there are always only two Sith at a time - a master and an apprentice. When Darth Maul died,

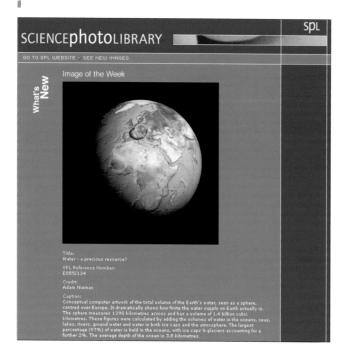

The two email ads illustrated on this page show that this is a medium that is suited to delivering information to a variety of audiences. The London-based Guardian newspaper email is designed to play on the fact that newspaper buyers will actually read the message.

StarWarsKids.com

June 6, 2002 © Issue # 36

re Background: The

nosis began in the pit of
na as Super Battle
pers and Jedi fought for
you the setting to
s. Click on the link to
appropriate for play and
is ink in your printer!

YODA

2

2
The Star Wars Kids mail is designed to appeal to children both young and not so young…. It is also more consciously designed to look like the full webpage, which Star Wars fans are likely to be heavy users of.

Prepare for spam

Most advertisers avoid the resultant bad feeling by making all email campaigns "opt in" rather than mandatory. Even the big service sites don't send out email shots automatically, as they appreciate the aggravation this can cause. However, when users personalize a portal, they are often unwittingly opening themselves up to blanket emails from companies that operate in customers' stated areas of interest.

There are, of course, added data protection issues

in most major online territories where the law states that they have to be opt-in. It is a fact of life, though, that many email ads are still unsolicited. The global reach of the Internet makes local regulation difficult, if not impossible.

But the benefits of emails remain numerous. If an email is in HTML format—that is, it looks like a webpage—then the obvious benefit is that it extends the reach of a website into the user's inbox. These so called "rich" emails can also be used to house video clips and other rich media such as you might find on an actual webpage. They can also carry forms and other feedback mechanisms. There is, however, the problem that the recipient's inbox could quickly become cluttered with large files or attachments. In comparison, a standard text-style email can only include a hyperlink and can contain no animation or interactivity other than the aforementioned links.

Rich email restrictions

The idea of rich emails is attractive but it does have one significant drawback. Most Web-based email services such as Hotmail do not support anything other than simple text emails. Programs like Microsoft's Outlook can display HTML-based rich emails, but services such as Hotmail haven't historically done so. This can reduce the impact of such a campaign, limiting it to office workers or users with access to a full email program rather than the millions who use Web-based email.

Hotmail, and other similar services, also tend to limit the size of the user's inbox, so bulky mailouts could cause the recipient storage and account problems.

Most email campaigns make use of a single link to get around this. If an email is sent out and opened in an inbox that can't display HTML, then a simple link is displayed that connects to a microsite that contains the same information as the email.

VIRAL CAMPAIGNS

One of the main techniques now being used for advertising on the Web is viral marketing. Put simply, it means that the message about the product or service is passed from user to user directly rather than by getting them to visit a site or look at a banner. It spreads like a virus from host to host, and in some cases it can change as it goes. This is very effective, because the recommendation regarding the product or ad comes not from a company but from users. This gives the campaign real credibility

Word of mouth
Viral campaigns exist in a variety of forms, but the most prevalent is simply a link that is sent around the email system. As previously discussed, John West launched an Internet-only campaign that consisted of a link to a site where a funny short film played. On first viewing, the film was funny enough to result in the link to the site being sent around the world via email.

Many others have tried to be this successful but not all have worked so well. Most viral campaigns have to have a real incentive for the viewer in order to get them to spread the word. Like real viruses, some prosper and some don't, and a badly executed campaign can do more damage to a brand than good. If it portrays the wrong message and gets out of control it is very difficult to stop. Once it's "out there," it has left your hands for good. Unlike a website or a TV ad, a viral campaign caanot simply be pulled "off air."

Good viral campaign designers take great care to create the artefacts in such a way that the mechanism by which they are transmitted is very simple. This is usually just a link, but it can also be embedded inside something else, such as an email. More successful campaigns can be transmitted as news items. If something catches the collective imagination, it is by no means uncommon for a link to the story, and by proxy to the campaign, to

1

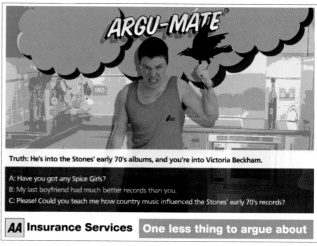

4

circulate worldwide on the Web within the space of two or three days.

When successful they are great examples of using what is unique about the Web. The ability to use peer-to-peer (P2P) networks via email is one of the Internet's great triumphs and viral marketing is the only form of advertising that really exploits this.

2

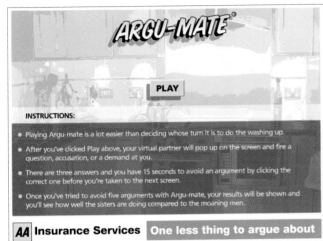

3

5

6

1 | 2 | 3 | 4 | 5 | 6

This viral campaign uses humor and the natural male/female competitiveness to give it its viral qualities. Men were supposed to pass it on so that the men came out on top and vice versa for the women.

All the time, the brand was gaining lots of exposure.

MICROSITES

The growing complexity of corporate websites and the limitations of banners meant that advertisers quickly found problems when wanting to provide a richer online experience, or convey a more complex message (as they would in traditional media). The search for more engaging and better-targeted advertising has lead not only to a massive increase in the use of games, but also the emergence of a new form of branded content, the microsite.

A microsite is a small website that exists for one specific purpose. It often contains no more than five or six pages. Usually a company will purchase a specific URL related to the promotion, and then build the site in a way that enhances the brand experience.

The content on the site is usually related specifically to whatever is being promoted—in other words, the site will carry only message-related content. So in the case of the Playstation2 game, Jak and Daxter, the URL and the content exist to allow users to experience the back story of the game, to view clips and download screensavers.

Mixed media

If a product is launched across a range of media, a microsite allows you to place as much accessible information as possible in one place. This enables your potential customers to find out more about the product quickly and easily. Retailers often use microsites for seasonal offers, to highlight specific goods out of a probable list of thousands of products.

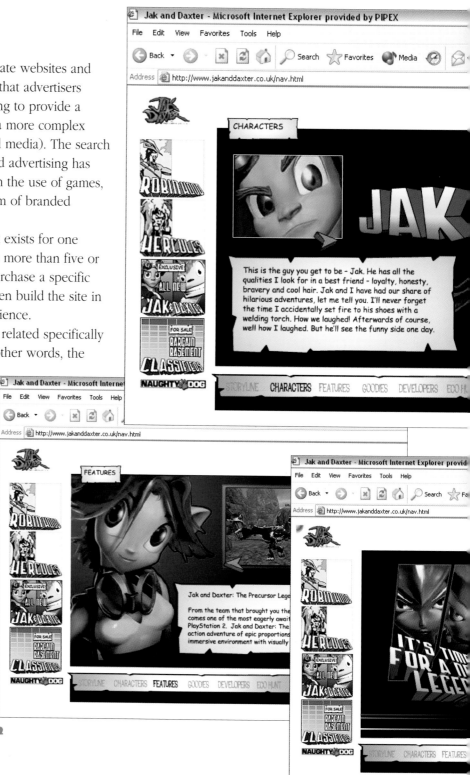

1

2

3

1 | 2 | 3 | 4

www.jakanddaxter.co.uk The user bypasses the main site and goes straight to the game site where they can read about the characters, the situations in the game, features and more. This being the Web, the site can

also act as focus for a community. Indeed, many Microsites do just that by having regular information updates, sending out emails to users, and by allowing users to engage in easy contact with other fans.

This approach has many advantages over banners and other standard online ad formats, not least of which is the fact that the brand experience and message can be fine-tuned to your requirements. You can add text to ram home your message, and perhaps a shopping basket as well for those all-important dollars, or a link for customer feedback. Furthermore, video, sound, and other rich media are all at your disposal to use in a more controlled and self-contained manner.

Getting seen

Of course, once you've built the site, you need to make your consumers aware of its existence. Try placing a link within your everyday emails. Obviously, you can throw traditional media into the mix to cross promote your microsite.

Be aware, though, when your campaign has run its course and be able to take down the site. Microsite-based campaigns have a limited shelf life. You need to think of them in the same way you would any other advertising campaign—they're "for a limited period only!"

Sony, again, makes good use of cross-promotion. Each Playstation2 game has its own microsite, each produced by a different agency, which gives consumers a direct experience of the game. These sites act as satellite sites to the main Playstation2 site, and mean that gamers can access content directly. They thus reflect the interest and richness of each game. When a game becomes obsolete, the site can be easily removed without having an impact on the main site.

109

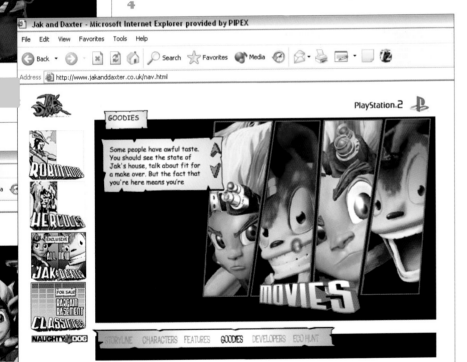

GAMES

In recent years there has been an explosion of online, branded games. Some studies forecast that the amount spent on advertising-related games will reach $1 billion by 2005 and that the vast majority of this will come from games that have brand messages directly embedded within the interactivity.

This is because one of the main problems with Web advertising is the user's willingness and ability to click away from the message. The medium actively encourages this by being based on hyperlinks. Games, however, present engaging and enticing content in a form that makes use of the unique interactive properties of digital media and encourages consumers to click on the advert (or game in this case).

Pros and cons

Through games, advertisers can initiate consumer interaction and then bring them back over and over again by use of competition and high-score tables. If a multiplayer game is built, then the brand message can be spread even further through peer to peer interaction. In fact many very successful games have been spread virally or through related product leverage, such as printing Web addresses on packaging. Prize games are also popular.

Research suggests that users spend much longer on gaming websites than they do on any other types of sites. Online games are particularly popular with young people, the market that appeals to most advertisers. According to analysts at investment bank Merrill Lynch, approximately 52 percent of online gamers are college age or less.

These factors are very important when deciding whether to use games as a way of advertising online. So what are the pitfalls? The cost of producing a good game can be high and, as with microsites, there are hosting, serving and maintenance costs to factor in. The maintenance of dealing with entries fairly and managing prizes can be costly and extensive too.

110

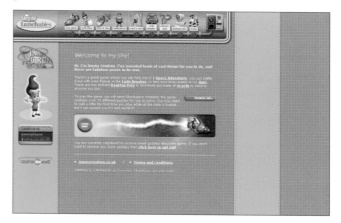

1 | 2 | 3 | 4 | 5 | 6 | 7

The introductory page of most game sites usually tries to explain what the game is and how good it is, so that users are enticed into the game.

The next page asks for personal information so that a user can be given a password. This is done for two reasons. First, the information is useful for marketing research. Second, the password allows tracking of individual usage to be implemented.

The user enters via a launch game screen. The game is downloaded at this point. The user can now choose which level to play the game at as well as reading rules and other related information.

The user now plays the game. After playing, the user can then access other fun and information.

2

3

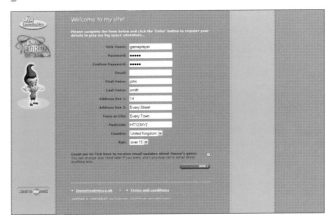

5

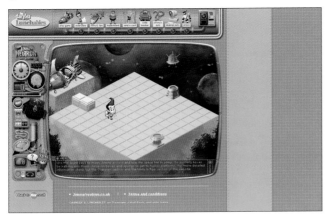

6

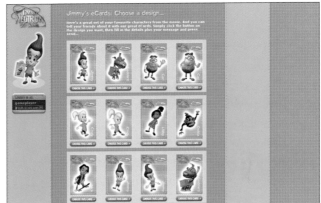

The main pitfall, however, is to assume that your brand needs a game. Clearly a game will suit certain brands more than others: sports-related brands are examples of a good fit; a furniture retailer is not.

In any game the nature of the interaction and gameplay is paramount. If a game is targeted at an audience that works all day in offices, the game should be playable quickly. If a longer experience is desired, the game should allow the playing to be interrupted and resumed at the same point. Again, the golden rule applies: know your audience!

7

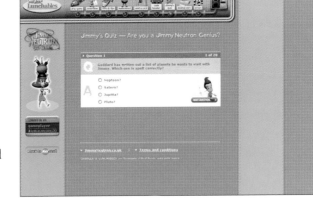

RICH MEDIA

Rich media is one of the fastest-growing areas of digital advertising—blending streaming sound and video with interactive features to dynamic effect. It relies on newer technologies that make it difficult for many users to access, and usually involves large file sizes, myriad plug-in formats, and memory-intensive presentations. But the sheer entertainment factor is compelling enough to attract large numbers of the right kind of viewers: those with money to spend.

The film industry has made this method its own, placing rich media within detailed, feature-packed microsites, alongside simpler content that "lo-fi" users can also access. Sign up for emails from a forthcoming film and when they arrive they will invariably contain links to trailers, or even, in some cases, trailers that start up immediately when the mail is opened or the microsite page is found.

Rich media can be very effective, but it is also expensive. Streaming video is not only difficult to edit and prepare, it also demands a great deal of bandwidth, and should ideally be run from a dedicated streaming server with specialist software (which is expensive in itself). The advertising host will be only too keen to pass this cost on to the client.

Drawbacks

Large downloads can also slow up a network and lead to complaints. If everyone in a company is viewing a video at the same time, then it will slow down the corporate network and can create all manner of secondary problems internally.

This is why streaming is central to using rich media. Streaming is a method of

2 | 3
In this example, for the third Austin Powers film, users can use rich media to view a trailer. Little other information is available. It simply acts as a teaser promotion for the product.

3

1
Film companies are undoubtedly the biggest users of rich media microsites. Such sites enable movie companies to preview films and advertise merchandise and release dates.

delivering video and audio in small packets of information as and when it is needed, rather than obliging you to download a huge file all at once. Real Player and Windows Media Player content is streamed.

The upside of rich media is that it is, to all intents and purposes, accurate in terms of reporting back on the number of downloads. An advert cannot be seen without linking to the server. It also carries a high impact factor. Who isn't impressed by video on their PC?

COOKIES

Cookies are essential in online advertising, as they provide a means for us to count how many times someone views a page, what route they take though a site, and whether they buy a product after clicking on one advertisement or another.

At times cookies have received a very bad press: people worry most about security and privacy, but these fears are largely due to a misunderstanding about what cookies do and how they work.

A cookie is a piece of information that a webpage asks the user's Web browser to store on their computer for future reference: this might include their name, user id, or log-in details, for example. A website can store as many of these as it likes, but it cannot directly access any part of the user's system, and it cannot get hold of personal or system information unless the user provides it.

How they work

The idea is that when you click through to another page on the same site, or return to the site again at a later date, the webpage can ask the browser what information has been stored, in order to remember your name, what page you were on last, or whether you showed an interest in a certain type of ad, for example.

Importantly, it's Web browsers that control cookies, not webpages, and they store these by domain name, in encoded format in a special file or folder. Webpages can't access cookies set by a different domain. Information remembered for one site is not remembered for another.

As any advertiser knows, facts and figures are key to driving the industry forward. Cookies have the important role of remembering a unique session id when someone comes to a site. This session id enables Web server technology to track how many pages the user looks at, how long they spend on each page, what wording and imagery attracts the most clicks, and, subsequently, what the broad interests of the site users are.

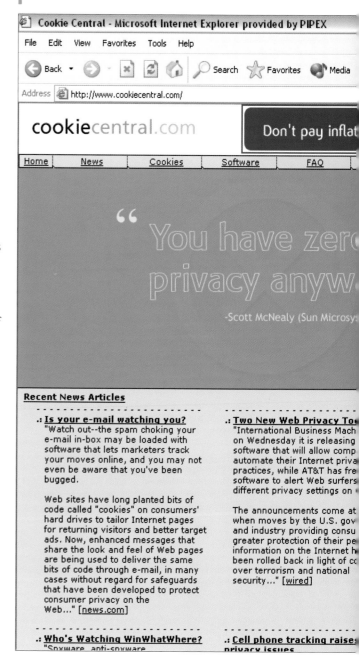

Cookies offer tremendous opportunities for the creative ad designer. If your ad is a viral campaign that includes a game, it would be of great benefit to you to be able to recognize your return visitors. A well-designed site can greet them by their nickname,

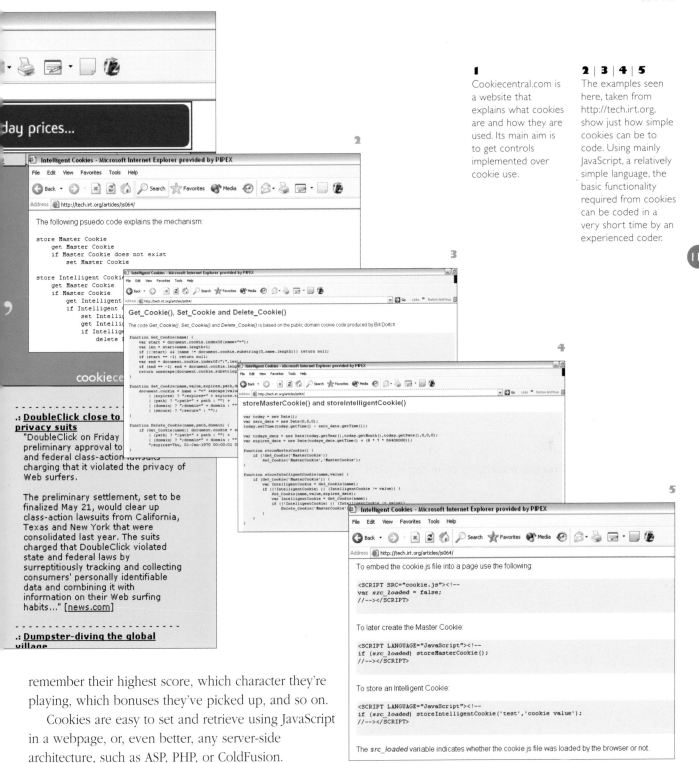

1
Cookiecentral.com is a website that explains what cookies are and how they are used. Its main aim is to get controls implemented over cookie use.

2 | 3 | 4 | 5
The examples seen here, taken from http://tech.irt.org, show just how simple cookies can be to code. Using mainly JavaScript, a relatively simple language, the basic functionality required from cookies can be coded in a very short time by an experienced coder.

115

remember their highest score, which character they're playing, which bonuses they've picked up, and so on.

Cookies are easy to set and retrieve using JavaScript in a webpage, or, even better, any server-side architecture, such as ASP, PHP, or ColdFusion.

BRANDED CONTENT

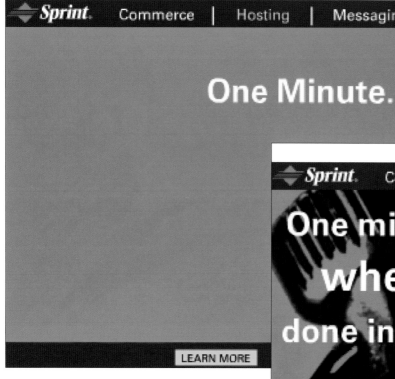

While the banner, pop-up, and other formats have been on the end of some considerable criticism from technologists and surfers, they have retained their place as the baseline of online advertising.

Combinations of faster connection speeds, tiredness of format and newer technologies have combined to create the conditions where a range of more complex, richer advertising solutions have emerged. This has begun to have some unexpected effects.

Out of the tidal wave of changes there has emerged a new form of ad that at the time of writing is still in fledgling form. This is the new phenomenon of branded content.

1
The ad presented here welcomes users to a piece of content that can help them learn more about particular services. The presentation and design is both serious and accessible.

2
The ad opens with a fully animated movie that gives information on what is in the application, enabling the user to click through. The information needs to be concise.

Branded content is content that is created by companies specifically to advertise products or communicate brand messages and this is turning into a major art form in itself. In order to give maximum value, companies as diverse as BMW and Kellogg's have all gone the branded content route and have begun to produce content ranging from short movies to interactive playgrounds. The unique feature of all these new approaches is that the games, movies, and other content is usually first-rate in quality and does not overtly advertise a particular product. In fact, given the rise of product placement in other media, it is becoming increasingly difficult to distinguish between content and advertisement. It is precisely at this frontier between advert and content that we are witnessing the birth of a new media form.

3
By presenting menu options on which a consumer can click, a mini application can be used to communicate a particular message easily and simply.

4
The end result is a cheap, effective piece of micro-content that both helps users and guides them to the main site. It is actually genuine content that acts as advertising.

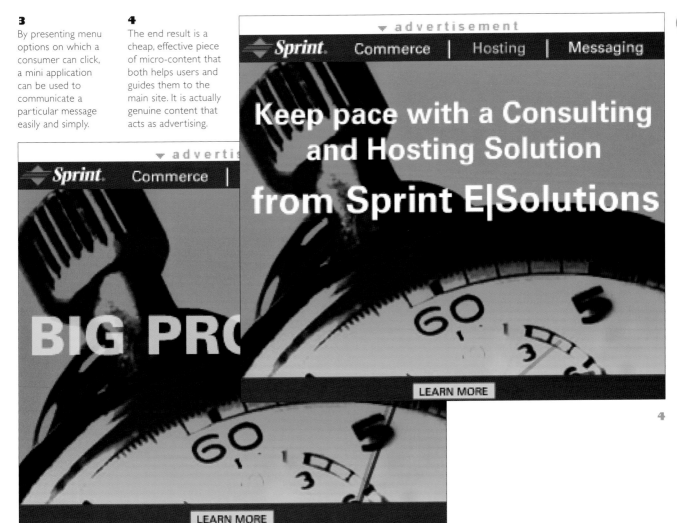

4

GAMES 1

The most visible form of branded content to emerge has been games. Companies have been keen to pursue games as an advertising tool for several reasons. Number one is that they are fun—and if you are fun then people tend to like you. For some brands, of course, this is not appropriate, but for most general household brands it can work very well.

FMCG brands can benefit enormously from this approach. The example shown here is for Hula Hoops "Shoks," a simple chip-like snack. The Hula Hoops game is typical of the increasing amounts of activity on the web aimed at younger audiences.

The game is typical in three ways. First, it is fun. Second, it links the fun to the brand, in this case by allowing users to see the related TV ads that were banned from being shown on TV before certain times of the evening (they were considered too strong for young children to see). Third, it encourages users to send on the ads in a viral fashion, thereby extending the life and reach of the campaign.

The game itself is made in Shockwave and, as discussed earlier, this is because this format allows for

2

3

1

1
The design of this superb online campaign is an extension of the offline and TV ads. A fun game is perfect for the target audience. Other content, such as banned TV ads, can also be included for viewing.

2 | 3
It is crucial that the game is designed not just as an attractive piece of content that keeps people on the microsite longer, but also as a brand or ad message extension; otherwise the effect will be lost. This game is an excellent example of this.

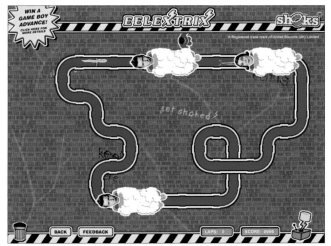

full feature games to be created. The game has controls that are easy to use, easy navigation, timers and a final score system. It also links nicely into a webpage.

This is a good example of an ad that has become content. The brand Shoks is aligned with content that reflects the "shock" nature of the name through the use of electric eels in the imagery.

More and more brands are using computer games to get their message across because more and more people are playing them. The Interactive Digital Software Association reckons that in the USA alone, 60 percent of all Americans play video games, which is actually about 145 million people. This market was worth $6.35 billion in U.S. entertainment software sales in 2001. Worldwide the figures are of course much larger.

It is clear, computer gaming is an established culture and more and more people of all ages and from all walks of life are involved in it. This makes it a prime marketing avenue and potentially a great advertising menu. Gamers are, however, notoriously sensitive to commercialism, which is why the brands have tried to access the culture through becoming part of it.

4
Games in ad campaigns tend to be simple and quick to play but also try to be addictive. Great emphasis is often placed on making the game fit the brand as well as making it fun.

5
When the game is complete, there should be a page that summarizes the experience, shows links to high scores and offers the player the chance to find out more.

6
If the game is an excellent experience, the user will send on an invite to play to another user. This has a viral effect and can help build an accurate database of user information.

121

GAMES 2

Games are such a powerful medium that they are also being used by brands that wouldn't normally even be associated with games. The previous example, "Shoks," was a fun brand aimed at young people, and games are easy to associate with this target market. The example here is slightly less obvious.

Virgin is a very successful umbrella brand that is used on products ranging from airlines through trains to, as shown here, mobile phones. All the products and services within the portfolio aim to reflect the Virgin brand values. The mobile phone service is aimed at people in the younger age range, who like stylish functional goods but also want good-value service. These values fit very well with the "Who Wants to be a Millionaire" TV show audience profile. A tie-up can be of immense benefit to both brands. The game shown here is a good example of how this type of branded content can use another complementary brand to achieve its aims.

Going mobile

The game allows users to play the game online as if on a mobile phone, or they can actually play via their data services carried by the phone service. In the case of the "Shoks" game, the game was combined with TV ads. This one brings the actual product onto the website and combines the game with mobile telephony. This is particularly effective in markets such as the UK, where a large percentage of the population already has mobile phones. It is a saturated market, which means that service and related values are very important to the brands within it.

Interestingly, again this game uses a viral mechanism to help it to extend its life and reach beyond the immediate targets. On the last screen of the game, a link is available to send the game to a friend. This is yet another example of a campaign that is using the inherent nature of the medium as opposed to trying to replicate existing media.

Inherent in games is a time factor that is very valuable to advertisers. Players join in with content that lasts for as long as they are kept engaged by the game. This provides a lot of brand or ad message visibility. If a quiz game is 15 questions long, there are five seconds to answer a question, then the player is exposed to the message for at least 75 seconds. This is three times as long as for a TV ad, an incredible length of time to get someone to view an ad.

2

1 | 2 | 3

All the classic game mechanisms are in use here. The microsite welcomes the user, the design clearly shows that the game is mobile phone-based, and the site always carries both brands. The design is clear and straightforward but very effective while also communicating the cross-media nature of the game. It shows what the user's experience on the phone will be and gives very clear instructions on how to join in. Superb ads such as this can be very successful.

123

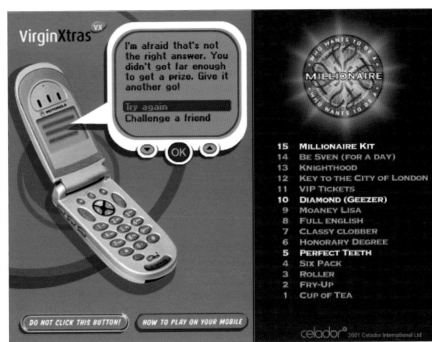

3

Games, as discussed before, are very engaging. Audiences love playing games. And although more than half of games' players are of college age or less, according to the IDSA website, 43 percent are women and the average age of an interactive game player is 28 years. These figures are often quite surprising to people when they first see them.

And while it is certainly true that computer and other digital games are more likely to be played by teenage boys, it is worth bearing in mind that TV game shows have proven time and again that women also love to play games and it should not be surprising therefore to learn that this is transferring to digital games. Similarly, the fact that the average age of players is 28 makes sense when it is considered that games are expensive, consoles and PCs are expensive and so players have to have money to buy them. Whether they are of working age or have brow-beaten parents is not entirely clear!

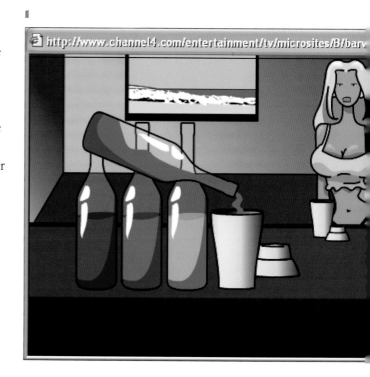

1

1
The game communicates to a wider range of people than might be normally expected from a game. The design reflects a "youth holiday" feel that is clearly aimed at a particular audience.

2
Simple graphics delivered in a straightforward, contemporary and fun way serve to reinforce that this ad is aimed at younger people who might vacation in destinations with lots of bars and clubs.

2

3

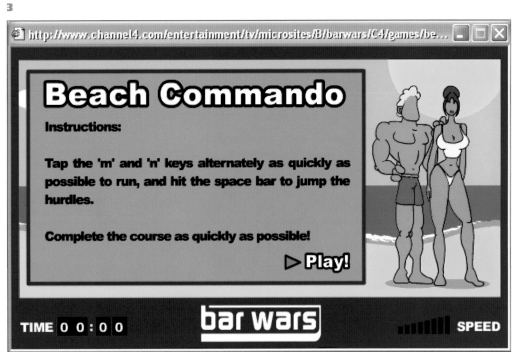

Beach Commando

Instructions:

Tap the 'm' and 'n' keys alternately as quickly as possible to run, and hit the space bar to jump the hurdles.

Complete the course as quickly as possible!

▷ **Play!**

TIME 0 0 : 0 0

bar wars

SPEED

125

TIME 1 1 : 1 1

bar wars

SPEED

3

Simple instructions and clear graphics reflect the fact that the audience for this game is not just hard-core gamers. It is important to get this right, so it is crucial to know the target audience.

4

The game itself is a simple entertainment concept. It also fits visually with the expected experience as built up by the previous screens. This reinforces the fact that you need to know your audience.

4

GAMES 3 (CONT)

5

5 | 6

Games are an excellent way to get people to interact with a site. Larger information or entertainment sites can make great use of them to keep people from moving off. In the case of TV channels, they can be used to reflect the nature of the content on the main site.

7

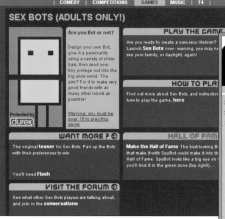

7 | 8

Sex can be used in games just as it is used in all other media. It's a common misconception that games are for kids only. In fact, many adults enjoy games and this should be borne in mind when commissioning and designing the content for a site where the aim is to engage the user and stop them moving on. If the audience is adult, the game can be adult.

8

The games shown here are used to add value to a UK TV channel's website. The amount of games here related to programs means that the website itself is becoming a destination in its own right and is beginning to take on a life of its own. The sole reason for this is to engage viewers in dialog with the brand, and gameplay is seen as crucial to this. While this is not strictly speaking advertising in its traditional sense, such a website is still advertising a product: the TV channel. It gives players a flavor of the programs they can watch on the TV channel, it extends the TV viewing experience and serves to reinforce brand value.

In this case the games are simple to play and are based around TV program contexts.

Large brands using games as content are engaging in activities similar to this TV station. They are beginning to produce content that is pure in form and exploits the uniqueness of interactive media.

If there is one thing that is unique about digital media it is the level and nature of the interactivity offered. Interactivity is king and this is why games have emerged as the predominant entertainment format. TV, radio and newspaper games simply cannot be as immersive and interactive as computer-based games. Neither do they have the ability to be spread virally. Interactive digital games and advertising have a long way to go yet, but the synergy is looking to be a deep and meaningful one.

9 | 10
Adult games are starting to appear on more mainstream sites as early scare stories about the Web die down. This means that there is room for adult games that advertise adult products, or in this case reinforce the message that the audience for the main site is adult.

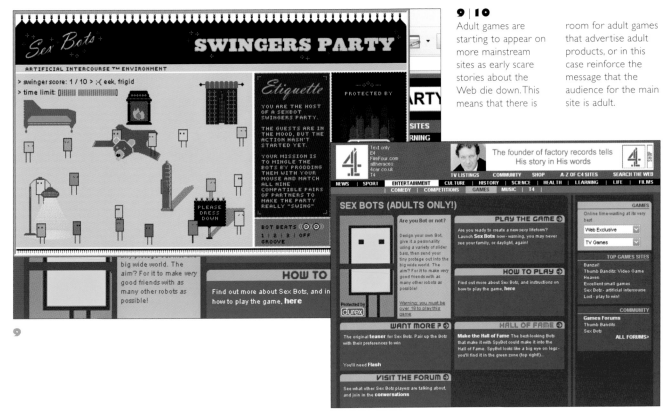

9

10

MICROSITES 1

When deciding whether to create a microsite, there are several issues to take into account. Over the next few sections we will explore some of these issues.

The first question to ask is whether this format is right for the product or message. An advertiser has to bear in mind that microsites are a more involving and richer experience, and so cost more to design and build than a set of banners. They also incur hosting costs and require maintenance, both technically and in terms of content, in order to be effective.

The film industry has, perhaps, been the major user of microsites, using them to promote the latest releases. Almost all major movies have their own microsite in order to build excitement in the run-up to a launch. The microsite allows information to be controllably and easily released stage by stage, as the studio wishes.

Using rich media, trailers can also be placed on the site so that users can watch or download them. In the case of the *Star Wars* and *Lord of the Rings* films, these trailers became viral objects in themselves. They were passed around the Web at great speed, which in turn served to build a sense of expectation and excitement among consumers. The microsite then provided a destination for all users who wanted further information.

In the case of more localized media, such as national TV and radio stations, much use is now being made of microsites that contain staged chat events with stars of the shows being broadcast. This is a very effective way of building loyalty and engaging the audience.

Clearly the big film and TV companies have good reason to want to build up excitement for a product: the risks involved in a film launching and then failing are vast. Their products are very desirable and glamorous in the eyes of the target audiences. They also have vast resources to call on in order to provide good content.

Not all companies have such glamorous products to sell. How, for instance, does a retailer use microsites in a similarly effective way when trying to sell more mundane day-to-day products?

1 | 2 | 3

Upon entering the *Lord of the Rings'* site, the user is presented with easy access to a range of supporting content based on the film. There are prominent links to trailers for the films and indeed new trailers are added regularly in order to enhance interest amongst users. All users can opt to receive emails informing them of developments and promotional items that they can purchase. The user can also click to see trailers for upcoming films and other video such as TV advertisements and interviews.

4 | 5

In the case of the new *Star Wars* movies, each has its own microsite that can be accessed from the main *Star Wars'* site. In common with other film sites, these carry links to trailers, merchandise and related content. Both sites are standalone, which means they can be easily removed and modified whenever the need arises.

MICROSITES 2

Microsites promoting household and electrical goods tend to be designed in a way that allows the consumer to become aware of pricing information and specific offers. For example, a company selling electrical appliances may well have a promotion that is designed to sell a specific set of TVs that in themselves are not glamorous products.

Timing

One strategy is to tie in the microsite with a seasonal offer. For instance, often after holiday periods, retailers will organize sales in order to encourage trade because consumer spending is low, disposable income having been spent on a holiday. In this case the most important message is likely to be pricing. The site will have to be changed regularly.

While the film and TV companies tend to produce very rich glossy experiences, retailers tend to be more focussed on communicating other messages. Designs will necessarily reflect the intended audience. A film or TV microsite will aim for an interest group based around the content, whereas a retailer might aim for a particular demographic group, such as children.

If we look at the example Kellogg's site, we can see that the design and layout are intended to appeal to a younger, family audience. The message is clearly about the brand values, and the visual design reflects this by being fun and clear but straightforward. The text in this case is written to appeal directly to children so that they can interact with the content easily. Long, complicated sentences are avoided. Jargon is only used where it is effective as a selling point on goods.

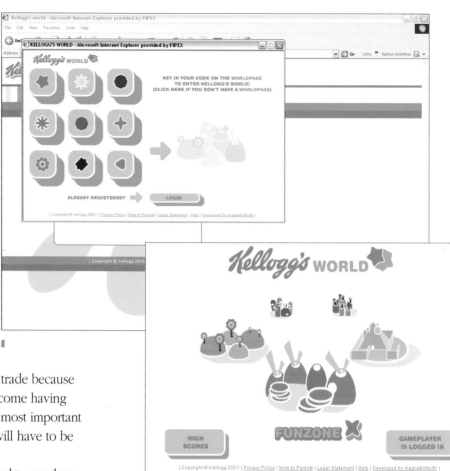

1

2

3

The other main use that retailers put microsites to is to gather information. Many retailers ask for personal information from users in order to be able to send them offers via email. In many ways this is a digital extension of standard direct marketing and customer relationship management techniques, and should be treated as such. Microsite information differs, however, in the fact that user information tends to be more up to date and provides a cheaper way of talking to the consumer. Using digital media also allows for personalization techniques to be applied in a more sophisticated manner than through using standard mail shots.

4 | 5 | 6
The user then accesses a menu that allows them to choose from a variety of content, including alpinegame, flowerzone, secretzone, space and others. The site is designed to offer a rich, engaging experience that will bring children back time and time again. This is a classic example of how traditional brands are becoming content providers under the auspices of marketing. To the main users, this is just a fun, interactive site. To the advertisers, the child is exposed to a genuine quality experience that helps reinforce brand values and gathers valuable data on customers.

131

4

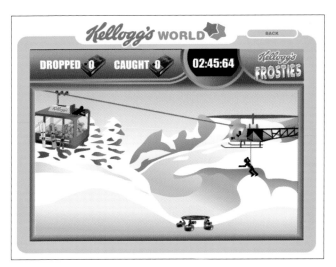

5

1 | 2 | 3
The user, following links read on related packaging and advertising, finds an entry screen. The user is asked to sign in and this is where marketing information on the user is collected. The clear incentive to signing in is the promise of cool, fun content.

6

VIDEO

In common with games and microsites, better technology and faster connectivity have made video via the Internet a reality. Earlier in the book we looked at bmwfilms.com, a site on which six short movies made by top directors are displayed. This is perhaps the best example of how content, branding and advertising are converging with digital media. This site uses Internet streaming technologies and faster connectivity to try and give users a taste of quality content.

BMW cars are considered to be high quality. The commissioned movies had to reflect this, so top directors and full-scale cinema crews were employed. The only constraint imposed on the movies was that they had to include some BMW cars. Other than that, they were to be first-class cinematic short movies.

The movies could be shown at cinemas or on TV and be considered to be of the highest quality. However, the Internet means that anyone can see them and there doesn't have to be costly distribution deals put in place. It is also significant that the whole experience of watching can then be tailored to reflect the brand experience. In this case, BMW have also provided their own viewer through which to watch the movies. As can be seen from the images, it provides a BMW logo link on the desktop which takes the user into a full screen immersive experience in which nothing other than the brand values are allowed to show through.

A campaign of this nature does require a significant investment but the viral effects have been enormous. This site has attracted

The international BMW films website

1

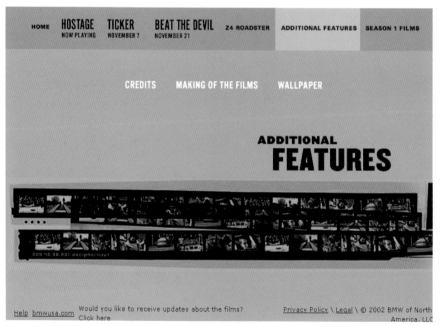

2

both admiring customers and the attentions of the advertising industry worldwide.

Merging branding and content doesn't get much better than this. This campaign is significant because it marks the line where traditional content, advertising and digital media really converge. Are the movies ads or are they movies? Does the fact they are distributed via the Web reduce or enhance their value? Few people can argue with the quality of the movies, and if they had been seen in cinemas first they would have been regarded as first-class shorts. This is where the excitement begins. This is the new advertising frontier.

1 | 2 | 3

Not content with a series of specially commissioned, big-budget movies to showcase its latest range of cars, BMW also produced a branded media player with which to watch them. While not every company can afford that sort of statement, many sites now feature video content. In the case of a big game like Grand Theft Auto III, clips of actual gameplay help showcase the visuals to potential buyers.

133

HOME | HOSTAGE NOW PLAYING | TICKER NOVEMBER 7 | BEAT THE DEVIL NOVEMBER 21 | Z4 ROADSTER | ADDITIONAL FEATURES | SEASON 1 FILMS

BMWFILMS.COM PRESENTS
THE HIRE
A SERIES OF SHORT FILMS

Brace yourself for a new season of intricate plot twists, riveting car chases, and a dose of wit. *The Hire*, a series of short films created by Hollywood's finest talent, is available here for downloading and streaming.

These brilliantly produced films star Clive Owen as the driver. Hired for his superb driving skills and unshakable poise, the driver encounters unexpected obstacles that put his abilities to the test.

ENHANCED FILMS

This format is how film enthusiasts can best view the films. Each Enhanced Film is a downloadable, high-quality, DVD-like experience.

ANGEL/BUFFY

These pop-ups demonstrate how sometimes a simple but beautifully rendered approach can be good. The soft coloration, combined with striking typography doesn't bombard the viewer with too much visual information. There is nothing flashy about these particular pop-ups, but the ads achieve good standout and are successful.

4

3

1

2

1 | 2 | 3 | 4
Despite the visually simple, uncluttered approach of the "Angel" pop-up, there are a suprising number of options available to click on.

5

137

5 | 6
This is almost an object lesson in the use of rollovers to dispense information in a quick, economical way. The advertised box set is broken down into tapes.

6

7
As users roll over the name of each tape a list of the episodes contained appears. This immediately whets the interest of the fan, and gives more casual users an impression of value.

7

ALI G

This campaign was set up to coincide with and promote a film release by the British comic character Ali G. Part of a nationwide and multiple media campaign, this online advertising makes use of a microsite combined with telephony to allow the user to engage in online karaoke.

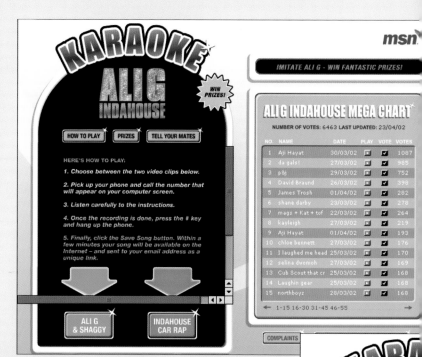

2

1

The home page of the Ali G karaoke site enables users that don't already have the ubiquitous Macromedia Flash, to download the software so they can continue through the site and play the game.

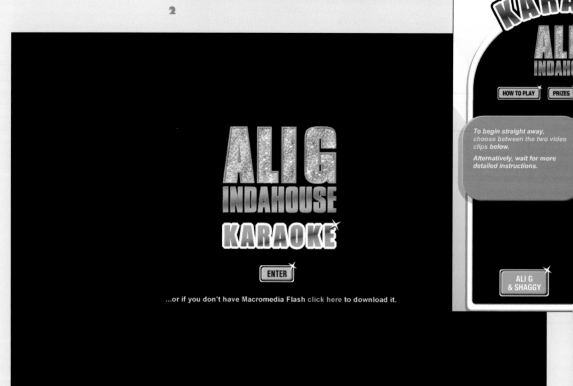

1

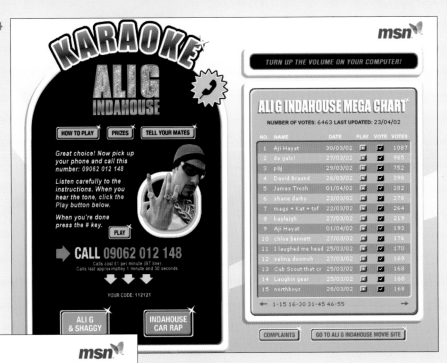

2 | 3

As users navigate through the site, there are various prompts that help them to record their impression entries.

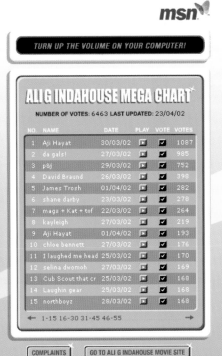

4 | 5

Once they have made and posted their recordings, users can log on to see their Ali G impression shooting up the karaoke chart. Of course the success of the campaign lies in the fact that users are encouraged to forward the URL to five of their friends.

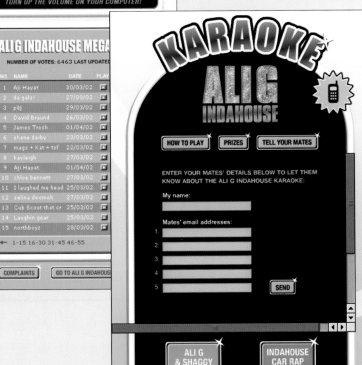

3

5

AUDI

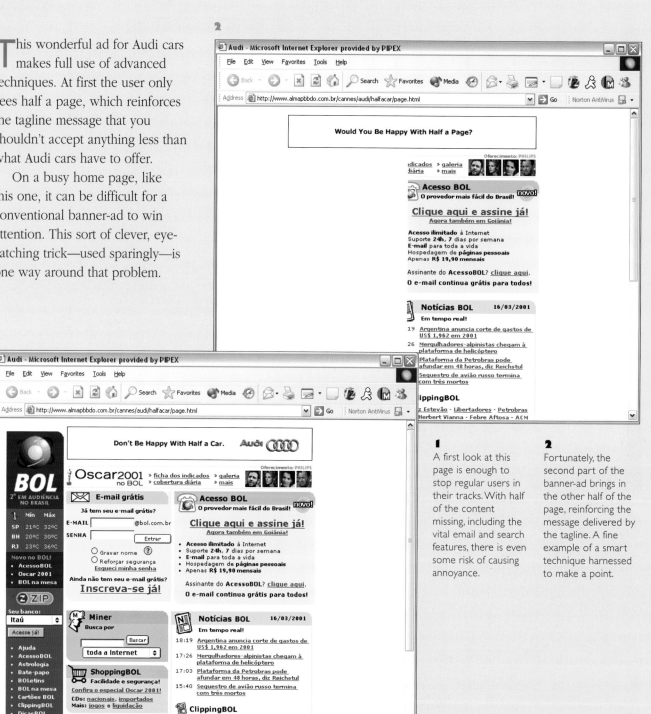

This wonderful ad for Audi cars makes full use of advanced techniques. At first the user only sees half a page, which reinforces the tagline message that you shouldn't accept anything less than what Audi cars have to offer.

On a busy home page, like this one, it can be difficult for a conventional banner-ad to win attention. This sort of clever, eye-catching trick—used sparingly—is one way around that problem.

1
A first look at this page is enough to stop regular users in their tracks. With half of the content missing, including the vital email and search features, there is even some risk of causing annoyance.

2
Fortunately, the second part of the banner-ad brings in the other half of the page, reinforcing the message delivered by the tagline. A fine example of a smart technique harnessed to make a point.

3

0.10

4

1.10

3 | 4
The use of animation in this banner is stunning. The speed with which the eye tracks the moving object communicates rapid acceleration.

5 | 6
By making the image an eye, the viewer immediately relates to what is actually happening—that the eye is watching the car accelerate.

5

2.20

6

4.58

7

The new Audi A6.
From 0 to 100 km/h in 5.20 seconds.

7 | 8 The second counter and the final text ground the basic impression of high performance in more specific terms. The numbers add weight to the message.

8

AUDI ⊙⊙⊙⊙

BACARDI

This is a great microsite from Bacardi for their Breezer product. The site encapsulates the nature of the product and the interactivity is simple and clean. The content is fun and highly interactive, allowing the viewer to watch TV commercials, play a game or even make their own video clip.

Part of the strength of this site is that it doesn't exist in a vacuum. It is closely tied in to a long-running TV advertising campaign and the brand's sponsorship of the UK hit show, Big Brother.

142

4

As the Breezer site promotes an alcoholic drink, it takes special measures to ensure that users are over Britain's legal drinking age. A Flash plug-in is also required.

2

Downloads offer the user more "meaty" content. Screensavers and "skins" for media player apps can give the product added visibility outside of the normal channels.

3

Like the screensavers, these email E-Cards use images from the TV commercials. The messages promote core values of the product: fun, friends, and relaxation.

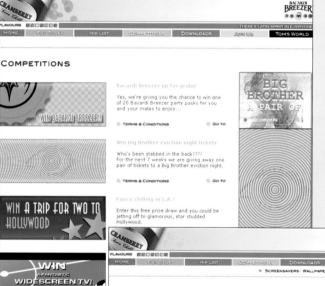

1

Competitions and prize draws attract new users to the site and provide a stream of information on those who enter. The choice of prizes also serves to strengthen brand values.

1

2

3

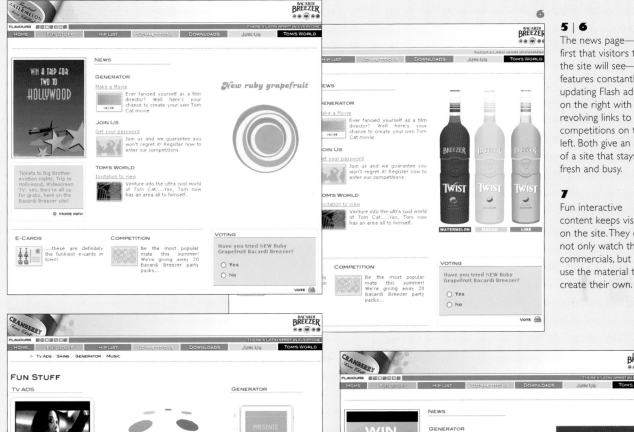

5 | 6

The news page—the first that visitors to the site will see—features constantly updating Flash ads on the right with revolving links to competitions on the left. Both give an idea of a site that stays fresh and busy.

7

Fun interactive content keeps visitors on the site. They can not only watch the TV commercials, but also use the material to create their own.

8

This section of the site works to push the alignment of the brand with the worlds of dance-music and clubbing, with live music direct from big club events.

9

The main colors used throughout the site are those of the flavors of Bacardi Breezer: the limited palette aids the clean style, while promoting brand identity.

BETINTERNET.COM

Simple, quirky ideas can sometimes be the most effecive. Betinternet.com, a sports gambling site, created this feature for the 2002 soccer World Cup. The Flash animations recreate classic moments of the tournament in the style of Subbuteo, a popular European table soccer game. The moments chosen are designed to appeal to a British audience.

1
The page gives users access to five classic World Cup moments from different eras. The choice enables the site to engage with visitors of different ages. Those who won't remember England's triumphant 1966 World Cup win should recall Michael Owen's 1998 goal.

2
The monochrome tones recapture the look of the original 1966 World Cup Final telecast. The rough graphics and table soccer style are a neat way of avoiding long downloads or bandwidth issues. File sizes can be kept down, but the results are still very effective.

3
The downside of the approach is that it does not leave much space or detail with which to characterize the different players. Note how the animator has worked around this, using small elements such as the hairstyles to identify the various participants.

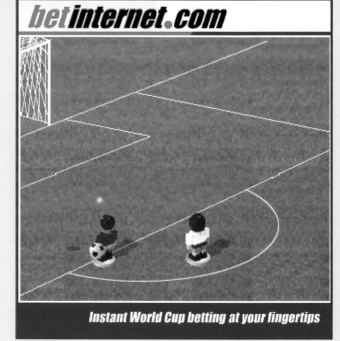

Instant World Cup betting at your fingertips

2

Classic World Cup Mini Moments

The winner of the World Cup final tickets has been contacted by email. Thanks to everyone who entered!

SEND THIS PAGE TO A FRIEND

THEY THINK IT'S ALL OVER — A model goal to clinch the 1966 final.

GORDON BANKS' INCREDIBLE SAVE — Banks gets all animated against Pele in 1970.

HAND OF GOD — The pint-sized wonder launches his netball career in 1986.

GAZZA'S TEARS — Featuring Gary Lineker's dazzling encrypted messaging skills in 1990.

OWEN'S GOAL AGAINST ARGENTINA — Simply sublime in 1998... more of this, please.

Click on individual clips to watch them! - Can't see the movies? Get the flash plugin

GO ON - BET ON ANY WORLD CUP MATCH NOW! — CLICK TO PLACE BET!

1

Instant World Cup betting at your fingertips

3

4

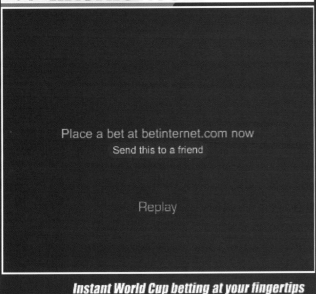

5

4
While this sort of idea is bound to win attention, the product branding still needs to be strong to capitalize on that interest. The logo at the top and the tagline at the bottom are obvious, but take note of the advertising boards separating the crowd from the play area.

5
For a campaign like this one to work, it needs to spread rapidly. Luckily, the use (and abuse) of email is now extremely common at work, and the "send this to a friend" link makes it simple for one user to pass word on to a friend or colleague in a matter of seconds.

6
Clicking on one of the smaller screens launches the pop-up, with a progress bar to indicate download progress. With larger Quicktime or Real Video files streaming would be a better option, but with small files the wait isn't long and the playback will be smoother.

6

3

2

Car manufacturers have been quick to embrace the marketting potential of the Web, and BMW has been more forward-thinking than most. The company's designers have mastered the art of producing eyecatching banners that exploit the small space for the maximum impact. The examples on this page combine simple ideas with bold visuals and clear messages. Within the confines of the banner format, less is definitely more.

With the most responsive steering ever

1

Clean, professional, slick and entirely in keeping with the brand values of the product, these banners are highly effective and communicate with a great deal of clarity and simplicity without ever losing their elegance and sophistication.

1

62-0 mph 2.6 sec

0-62 mph 5.2 sec

Quick thinking from BMW

The BMW M3

www.bmw.co.uk

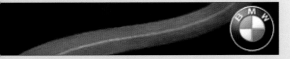

2
This banner takes the limited size of the format as a strength, pulling back from the car to reveal tracks in the shape of a fingerprint. This is a great example of using a subtle visual pun to push home the message in a more intelligent way.

3
Another advantage of the minimalist style used by BMW in these banners is that the amount of plain white (or black) space helps to keep the file sizes down. The more complex or colorful a banner is, the longer it will take some users to load.

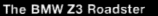

Stay fastened to the road

The BMW Z3 Roadster

www.bmw.co.uk

The BMW 3 Series handles

like it's a part of you

The BMW 3 Series

BMW MOVIE PLAYER

To go with their movie site, BMW also produced their own custom movie player to play the movies in as large a format as possible on screen. The player allows users to view the movies, find out who the directors are and—more crucially— get information about the BMW range of cars. This whole concept is second to none in its thoroughness and in the way it has made the maximum benefit from digital media as an advertising medium.

1
While the BMW films are enjoyable in their own right, the point is to showcase the cars. This section of the site closely maintains the techno style of the whole campaign.

2
Rather than overwhelm the user with technical spefications, the "featured machines" section provides a more stylish and readable overview.

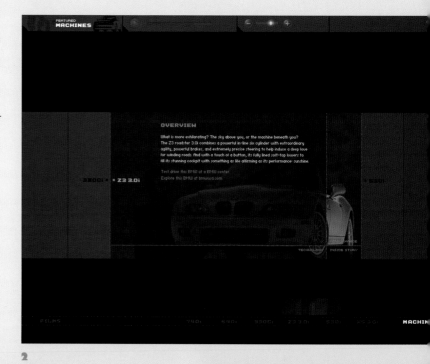

2

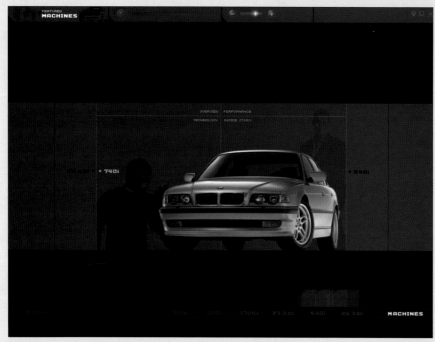

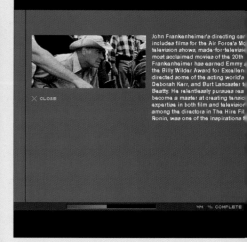

3
Each of the short movies was made by a big-name cinema director. As this is an important part of the campaign, each director gets a short biography detailing their most important achievments.

1

4

4
The "behind the scenes" material includes the driving techniques used in the various car chase sequences. This sort of content appeals to both car and film enthusiasts alike, while also pushing the message that BMW's advanced engineering made it possible.

5
Quality has always been limited when it comes to the presentation of movies on the Web, prompting BMW to create their own large-format player to show them. To view the movies at this size demands the luxury of a fast Interet connection.

149

5

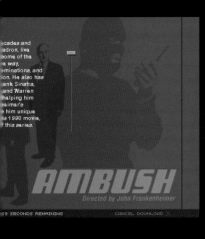

3

BMW MOVIE PLAYER 2

7

The use of a recognizable star was just as important as the choice of director. The British actor, Clive Owen, has the class and charisma to do justice to the BMW brand, but comes without the multimillion dollar paycheck of a leading Hollywood player.

6

6

To encourage more users to download the films, the site provides a brief synopsis, a trailer, and a choice of file sizes. Users with modem connections may still balk at a 23MB download, but the larger 78MB version is a broadband-only luxury.

7

8

The site contains a wealth of content, including all the movies and "behind the scenes" material. The interface, however, is quite simple. You can access each movie from the bar at the bottom, while the main screen includes explanatory text and options.

9 — 15

The selection bar at the bottom of the screen uses rollovers to give the name of the movie and the featured director. The fact that BMW had gained the services of big Hollywood names (John Frankenheimer and David Fincher), acclaimed international directors (Ang Lee and Guy Richie) and left-field figures (Wong Kar-Wai) was a key part of the campaign's wide-ranging appeal.

151

8

9

10

13

11

14

12

15

BT OPENWORLD

This clever pop-up plays on the assumption that users of old-fashioned modem connections will spend most of their time waiting for a page to download or update. While the ad says "watch this space" it is clear that nothing at all is happening. With a broadband connection, however, the user would get to the end up to ten times faster. This example is effective precisely because it works within the percieved limitations of the Internet as a broadcasting medium.

1 | 2 | 3 | 4

If you are trying to spot the differences, there aren't any! The whole point of this cunning pop-up is that, if you're surfing the Web on a regular Internet connection, you spend most of your time waiting for something to happen. If you want a little more excitement, broadband is the only way to go. While this is hardly the most thrilling advert on the Web, it certainly makes its point.

1

2

153

3

4

CULT FILMS

A super interactive ad that makes the point that there are more types of movie out there than just Hollywood blockbusters. It reinforces the perception that such movies are formulaic and predictable by allowing the user to create their own story, using simple pull-down menus that highlight how simplistic such scripts can often be.

Having created their generic story, the user arrives at the final, screen, which encourages them to try something more original.

154

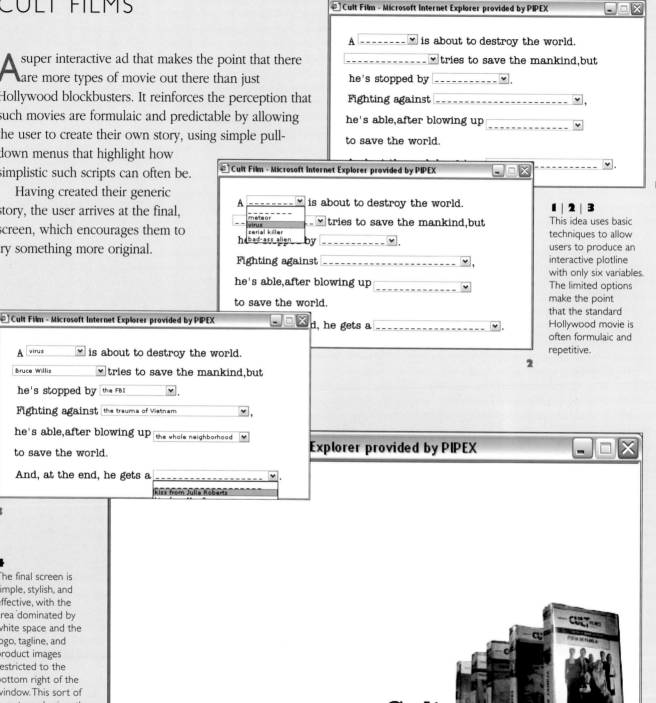

1 | 2 | 3
This idea uses basic techniques to allow users to produce an interactive plotline with only six variables. The limited options make the point that the standard Hollywood movie is often formulaic and repetitive.

2

3

4
The final screen is simple, stylish, and effective, with the area dominated by white space and the logo, tagline, and product images restricted to the bottom right of the window. This sort of layout emphasizes the quirky, offbeat nature of the brand and the films concerned.

Cult
Hey, see an original movie.

4

5
This ad for the Nintendo Gamecube games console shows how clever use of DHTML content can be used to surprise the user, with the glass box—a recurring feature of the Gamecube TV commercials—appearing to burst through the page and into the screen itself.

6
It is the details that make this animation so successful. The shattered glass and the discoloration beneath the break create an impression of a broken screen.

155

7
Having won the user's attention, the pop-up transforms into a countdown to the console's launch. During the period before release this would have built anticipation among the game's enthusiasts who would typically use this website.

THE GREEN PARTY

With conventional advertising so expensive, Britain's Green Party looked to the Internet for a means of communication. To this end, a group known as The Garden created a series of short films to be viewed and pass around on the Web. In these films, thought-provoking images combine with clear, factual voiceovers to raise concern over environmental issues. As word spreads fast on the Internet, such online, viral-marketing campaigns can become very successful.

2

1
The campaign was run with the help of the online marketing specialists, DMC. While viral marketing campaigns rely on word of mouth for success, DMC's online tracking systems enabled the Green Party to gather data on how many users were viewing the films, and how many were sending them on to friends.

2
For films to spread around via email or Web links, download times need to be kept to a minimum. As a result, all of the films had to be kept quite short (running for 30 to 60 seconds) and each needed to have visual impact within a fairly small playback window. These constraints presented the filmmakers with a tough challenge.

3

4

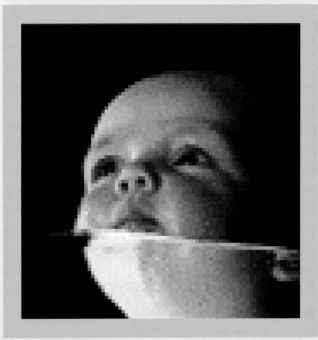

157

5

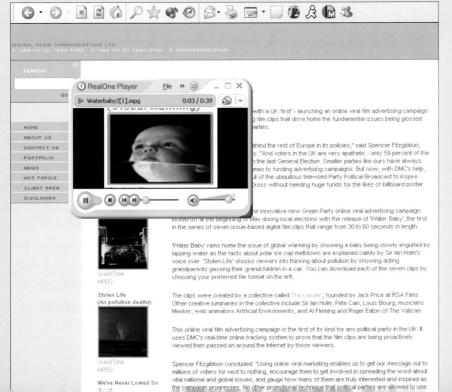

3 | 4
The Garden settled on distinctive images with a degree of shock impact. In *Water Baby*, an infant faces rising water levels while a voice explains the facts about polar ice cap meltdown. In *Stolen Life*, grandparents are shown obliviously gassing their much-loved grandchildren to illustrate the threat of air pollution.

5
For an online viral marketing campaign of this type, file formats are another prime consideration. Apple's Quicktime format is very widely used, but not every user will have downloaded the Quicktime viewer application. For this reason, the films are available in both Quicktime MOV and MPEG formats.

BRILLIANT INDUSTRIES

Egg, the UK financial services company, produced this website to work with a television commercial campaign. The commercials showcase Brilliant Industries, a fictitious company that produces ludicrous gadgets which claim to help their gullible buyers avoid debt or get rich. Egg provides a more sensible alternative. This microsite is a perfect example of how a good Web presence can back up an inspired TV campaign, expanding the list of products used in the commercials with even more ridiculous inventions. Interactive email-based elements add to the fun. The extravagant style has been cribbed from home shopping junk-mail, magazine supplements, and TV programs.

1

A key strength of this campaign is its creation of a complete corporate identity for Brilliant Industries, covering everything from the intro page (shown here) to the logos, colors, and button styles used within. This sort of joke works best when the fake company is almost on the verge of being plausible.

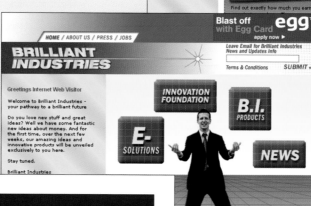

2

The main page has all the features you would expect from a company website, including "press" and "jobs" sections in the top bar. Only the Egg banner (*top right*) indicates the real purpose of the site.

3

The E-Solutions page contains a number of fun, interactive applets which fit in with the general Brilliant Industries mentality. Note that the interface remains consistent from page to page, with the sidebar changing to reflect where the user is on the site.

4

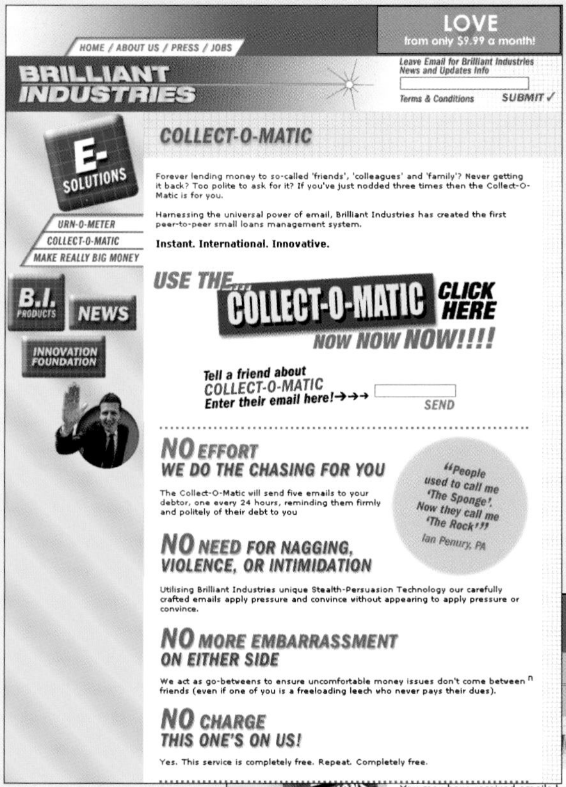

LOVE
from only $9.99 a month!

Leave Email for Brilliant Industries
News and Updates Info

Terms & Conditions   SUBMIT ✓

HOME / ABOUT US / PRESS / JOBS

BRILLIANT INDUSTRIES

E-SOLUTIONS
URN-O-METER
COLLECT-O-MATIC
MAKE REALLY BIG MONEY

B.I. PRODUCTS   NEWS

INNOVATION FOUNDATION

COLLECT-O-MATIC

Forever lending money to so-called 'friends', 'colleagues' and 'family'? Never getting it back? Too polite to ask for it? If you've just nodded three times then the Collect-O-Matic is for you.

Harnessing the universal power of email, Brilliant Industries has created the first peer-to-peer small loans management system.

Instant. International. Innovative.

USE THE... **COLLECT-O-MATIC** CLICK HERE
NOW NOW NOW!!!!

Tell a friend about
COLLECT-O-MATIC
Enter their email here!→→→ [   ] SEND

NO EFFORT
WE DO THE CHASING FOR YOU

The Collect-O-Matic will send five emails to your debtor, one every 24 hours, reminding them firmly and politely of their debt to you

"People used to call me 'The Sponge'. Now they call me 'The Rock'!"
Ian Penury, PA

NO NEED FOR NAGGING, VIOLENCE, OR INTIMIDATION

Utilising Brilliant Industries unique Stealth-Persuasion Technology our carefully crafted emails apply pressure and convince without appearing to apply pressure or convince.

NO MORE EMBARRASSMENT ON EITHER SIDE

We act as go-betweens to ensure uncomfortable money issues don't come between friends (even if one of you is a freeloading leech who never pays their dues).

NO CHARGE
THIS ONE'S ON US!

Yes. This service is completely free. Repeat. Completely free.

LOVE
from only $9.99 a month!

Leave Email for Brilliant Industries
News and Updates Info

Terms & Conditions   SUBMIT ✓

SOLUTIONS
URN-O-METER
COLLECT-O-MATIC
MAKE REALLY BIG MONEY

B.I. PRODUCTS   NEWS

INNOVATION FOUNDATION

IG MONEY

You may have received emails bragging how you can make big money working from home. Well now you really can with BI's most recent innovation - **Big Money Technology.**

If you think this is some kind of mail order chain letter postal pyramid spam scheme then you are wrong. Very wrong. This is a bona-fide, top class, first rate, no strings attached big money making system.

Making huge wads of cash has never been easier!

MAKE REALLY BIG MONEY CLICK NOW

Tell a friend about
REALLY BIG MONEY
Enter their email here!→→→ [   ] SEND

ANYONE

No training or special schooling is necessary. You can be any age, any sex, and have any kind of employment history. Even a criminal one!

ANYHOW

All you need is access to a computer - PC or Mac - and a digital photograph of yourself. That's it. No special equipment or tools are required.

ANYWHERE

In your living room, in your toilet, in your garage, on a mountain, in the sea. Thanks to the Internet, you can make big money anywhere on planet Earth.

ANYTIME

Make money when you want and at your own pace. Big Money is quick and easy to use. And you can go from nought to stinking rich in under 60 seconds.

ANY TAKERS?

HOME / ABOUT US / PRESS / JOBS

0% to 1/1/2003 on balance transfers,
12.6% APR (variable)

Leave Email for Brilliant Industries
News and Updates Info

Terms & Conditions   SUBMIT ✓

BRILLIANT INDUSTRIES

B.I. PRODUCTS

LA-LA FINGERS
IDENTITY RE-INVENTION KIT
MAGNETIC PENNY DETECTING FOOTWEAR
TELEPATHIC GOATS
CHEQUE DELIVERY MISSILE
OTHERS... & MORE

INNOVATION FOUNDATION

NEWS   E-SOLUTIONS

VIRTUAL SOLUTIONS FOR A VIRTUAL WORLD

Welcome to the nerve centre of Brilliant Industries. Our unique products show you new ways of looking at your money situation and provide new ways of dealing with those unexpected blows your finances tend to rain down on you at every turn. Each fantastic product, we believe, is the embodiment of our company mantra: "ideas ideas ideas ideas ideas ideas"

TELEPATHIC GOATS!

Introducing a new way to co-ordinate your finances and obtain milk. Click Here Turn cashmere into cash more!

MAGNETIC PENNY DETECTING FOOTWEAR!

Stride your way into riches with our money attracting boots – a GIANT leap forwards in wealth creation **Click Here**

IDENTITY RE-INVENTION KIT

brave face on debt. Not yours! Somebody else's. **Click Here**

MUSICAL FINGERS!

t your debts forever in a world of music and song **Click Here**

Industries
the Martini of Invention

4

One of these E-Solutions is the "Collect-o-matic." This sort of email-based service is a bit of fun content for the user, while the emails sent from them will encourage others to visit the site.

5

Like most of the site's content, the "Make Really Big Money" interactive feature strengthens the concept of Brilliant Industries that has already been delivered through the TV commercials, with content tailored to the capabilities of the Internet.

6

The Products page ties in closely to the original TV commercials, showcasing items such as the "La-La Musical Fingers" which have already appeared in the ads. Others, such as the fascinating "Telepathic Goats" appear here for the first and (thankfully) only time.

5

6

IVILLAGE

This is a great example of a site that allows full use of DHTML for ads. All the advertisers are making full use of the technology's capabilities to produce ads that walk and move across the page.

This approach has some clear advantages: the ads can be quite mobile, they can interact with the page, and they can employ dramatic or witty special effects. At the same time, if this type of DHTML ad is overused those strengths can become weaknesses. As the ads can interfere with the user's reading of the page, they may be something of an annoyance. Luckily, on this website the ads are imaginative, eye-catching and just another part of the fun.

1
This DHTML pop-up appears in the guise of an SMS text message. It grabs the user's attention, but its placement and transparent background ensures that it does not obscure the content of the site behind.

2
The blue bubble pop-up ties in to the O$_2$ mobile telephone network—blue bubbles are a regular theme in O$_2$'s corporate branding. The effect isn't subtle, but it's still less annoying than the average pop-up.

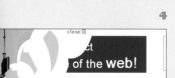

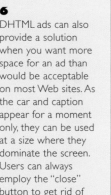

3

Using DHTML enables this sort of ad to—literally in this case—jump out of the box. Note how the loop of the bungie chord trails down over the page.

4

The bungie-jumper leaps out of the hoist and drops towards the bottom of the screen, narrowly missing before being pulled back up. This effective ad stands out from the rest of the page, but it also interacts with it in a way that is certain to catch the user's eye.

5

When DHTML ads appear overlaid on the page, as they do in this example, it can be a challenge to make smaller elements stand out from the background. This one gets past that problem through the use of bright colors and strong borders.

6

DHTML ads can also provide a solution when you want more space for an ad than would be acceptable on most Web sites. As the car and caption appear for a moment only, they can be used at a size where they dominate the screen. Users can always employ the "close" button to get rid of the ad more rapidly.

161

LAND ROVER

This advanced pop-up for the 2003 Land Rover Discovery is another ad that practically demands the user's attention. It acts as a "teaser," opening with a small, unidentifiable detail to reveal a bold image that aims to leave the user wanting more information. It works particularly well in the context of this page—the website of a popular British motoring magazine—as it can be safely assumed that the majority of users will have some interest in the product.

1
The pop-up first appears as a blob of image surrounded by a graduated brown fog. This immediately engages the user's curiosity. As the image starts with a small detail, it's difficult to see what is emerging from the screen.

2
The opacity of the brown fog increases and it solidifies into a rectangular space. At the same time, the image increases to reveal more—a headlamp and a portion of a radiator grille—but the user is still kept guessing.

3

3
This next stage uncovers another vital clue: a portion of the Land Rover logo. The heavy grille and square headlamps are also strong elements of the brand identity.

4
This frame ends the mystery with the simple message "New 2003 Discovery." The minimal level of information is very deliberate, as the intention is to create interest in the updated model. Neither the text nor the image gives any specific detail away.

5
Having made its point the ad shrinks down to a less obtrusive size, ready for the user to click through or close. This thoughtful final touch helps the ad to avoid any possibility of overstaying its welcome.

NIKE FOOTBALL

This game site is a direct tie in with a successful series of TV commercials in which some of the world's top soccer (or football, as the game is known in the UK) players are engaged in a secret underground tournament. The game format allows the users to directly participate. The design replicates the gritty, industrial look of the ads, and connects with the target audience brilliantly. The combination of Flash games, star players and Nike's strong brand values make this another great microsite.

3

1

4
Flash is also used to produce animations based on the action of the ad campaign, giving the user the chance to see football heroes in action.

5
The site's major draw is a 3D football game, which can be played either alone or online in a prize tournament.

6
Those playing the game can choose from the any of the three-man teams featured in the commercials, or can create their own from the individual players. As Nike works with so many of the world's best players, the game should appeal to users from the vast majority of footballing nations.

1
Nike has packed this microsite with tangible content, adding Flash games, screensavers, movie clips and wallpapers to the usual product showcase areas.

2
Every aspect of the site has been designed to capture the feel of the original ad campaign. This intro sequence relates the story behind "the secret tournament."

3
Using Flash as the backbone of the site has enabled a richer visual design. Note how cleverly the interface merges in with the frame at the top of the screen.

2

4

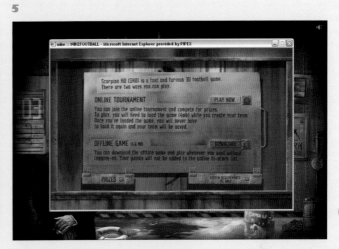

5

6

SCOOBY DOO

Hollywood has always been at the forefront when it comes to using microsites to promote the latest product. This comprehensive and rich example was created as part of the marketing campaign for the 2002 summer blockbuster *Scooby Doo*. It makes effective use of the design elements used in other, cross-media promotional activities, and has fun sections for each character, including a variety of games and other downloads. The movie was a big summer hit, especially with younger audiences.

166

2
This section leads to individual areas for each member of the Scooby-Doo gang, all packed with content appropriate to the character.

3 | 4 | 5 | 6
Shaggy and Scooby have games, a fun translator applet and a screensaver, while Daphne has her own photos and "Fight for Fashion" game.

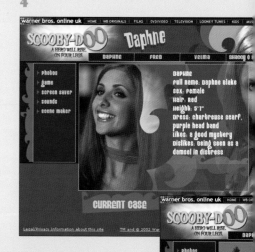

1
The site takes its strong visual style from the film, taking basic elements from the original cartoon series, then mixing and matching various influences from the 1960s and the present day. modern looks. The result is colorful, brash and very busy, but in a way that should appeal to the youthful target audience.

2

7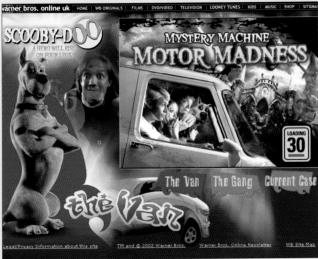

8

9

7 | 8 | 9 Users can also enjoy this Mystery Machine game. It is relatively simple stuff, but that is often a strength in this context. Again, the designers have been careful to make sure that everything fits in with the look of the movie.

10 This ghoulish section has been designed to match the gothic style of the Spooky Island location in the movie. It contains trailers, posters and news on the film, plus some material aimed at fans of the original cartoon series.

5

6

10

PUMA

This microsite from Puma is a very rich experience that combines interactivity, fun, and product messages. The Japanese theming of the Shudoh product range is reflected in a design that is heavily influenced by Japanese animation styles. This approach does not just give the site a strong look, it is also a natural match to the Flash technology used to drive it, keeping file sizes and download times down to a minimum.

2

1

3

1
The minimal interface, clean lines and cartoon style lend the site a dynamic feel that fits perfectly with the branding of the new product line.

2
Those design strengths continue in this stripped-back product showcase. The lack of clutter leaves the emphasis on the tagline and the boot itself.

3
As this site ran during the 2002 Soccer World Cup, it also references Puma's sponsorship of the plucky team from Cameroon.

4
Even this competition is an example of great design, with the background showing through the semi-transparent windows and photo thumbnails illustrating the prize.

5
The competition uses Flash to allow users to create their own custom boot: a fun idea that fits well with the "No Limits. Only Choices" concept.

4

6 | 7
The site also uses Flash for this amusing fighting game, based on the classic arcade machine, Streetfighter. Users with time to kill can battle it out as one of several Puma sponsored soccer stars in a comic sushi-bar brawl.

8 | 9
For this sort of Flash game neither the graphics nor the game controls need to be particularly sophisticated. Simple visuals keep the download times low, while basic gameplay makes the game easy to pick up and enjoy.

10
Like other forms of advertising, a microsite can use repetition to ensure that the message is received. Note how the site regularly refers to concepts such as "the master of soccer" and the "No Limits. Only Choices" tagline.

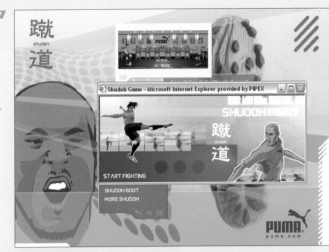

7

5

8

9

6

10

SHOKS

This ad, for the Hula-Hoops Shoks snackfood, shows that Web-based advertising can be every bit as provocative as anything seen on TV or in print. The designers have been given free rein to use the whole screen, with the naked bather fleeing from her bath and the brightly colored eels leaping out of the bath to menace the page entire.

2

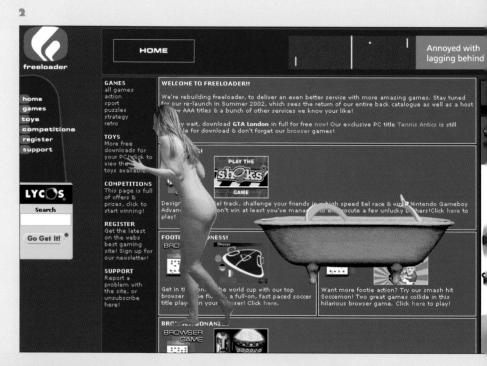

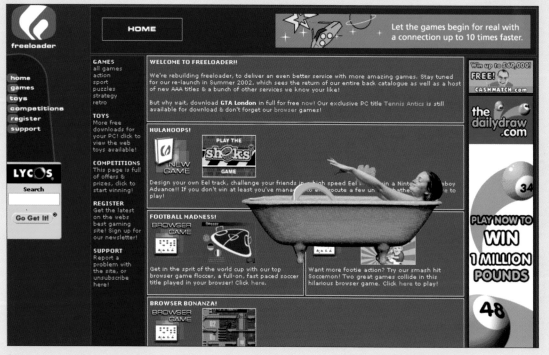

1

1 | 2 | 3

This Flash pop-up mixes bitmap and vector elements to great effect. The woman bathing is a bitmap graphic, while the two eels are highly scalable vectors. While the imagery is slightly racy—the bather is naked after all—this fits in with the risky, mould-breaking impression that the brand is attempting to present.

3

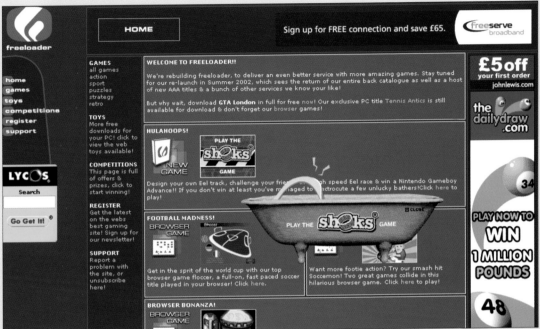

Having menaced the innocent bather, the eels now turn their attention to the rest of the page, escaping from the confines of the tub to attack the screen in general. Flash's vector-based animation capabilities are perfect for this example, defining the snakes in a few colorful strokes and allowing them to grow to such alarming proportions without creating large files or looking crude and blocky when so greatly enlarged.

4

5

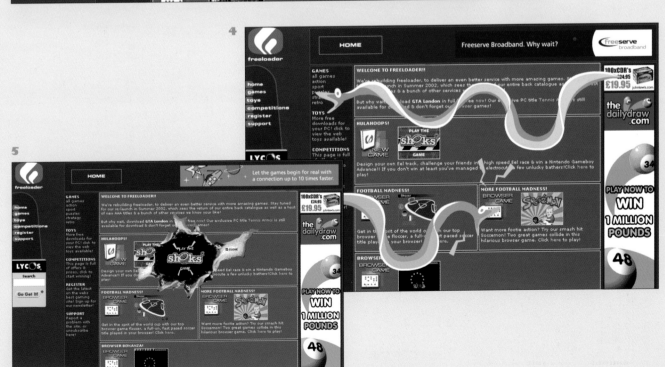

SMIRNOFF

Games should not be restricted to advertising kid-friendly products. As this Smirnoff effort proves, they can also work well in a more adult context. Like many companys in the alcoholic drink market, Smirnoff works hard to promote links with the cool clubbing scene, and this Shockwave applet uses music from leading international DJs as the soundtrack for a simple dance game. At the end, users can enter a prize draw to win CDs, clubbing trips, and festival tickets. The game was designed to back up a UK promotional campaign.

172

End of Level 1

level

.00

Switched On Dance

Keep the dancer making funky moves until you reach the end. Make it or not, you can win a range of cool prizes, including Glastonbury tickets!

Also, check out the Switched On promotion running in venues all over the country. Search for your nearest venue at the end and find out how to get your hands on even more prizes.

Warning - you need to be over 18 and live in the UK to play this groovy game!

1 | 2

The clear, fuss-free design gives every element of the game a feel of understated cool, while the style of play has been cribbed from a successful genre of arcade and console video games. Both the instructions (press the keys in the right order at the right time) and the objectives (keep dancing until the time is up) are kept deliberately simple to make the game easy to pick up and play: this sort of game works best if it is instantly accessible and highly addictive.

Instructions

7	8	9
4	5	6
1	2	3

What to do!
• Keep the dancer making funky moves until your time is up. Manage this and move up a club floor to dance to the next DJ
• Make it or not, you can enter into the prize draw to win Switched On prizes.

How to do it!
• Make sure you've got Num Lock pressed
• Use the keys 1-9 as shown to make the dancer move
• Press these keys in the correct order as shown on the left of the screen
• Press the correct key before the move disappears off the bottom
• The speed will increase, so you'll have to keep up!
• You have 3 lives to dance through four different DJ sets. Good luck...

level

.00

Instructions
Play

2

level

.01

tall paul

3
The visual design is tightly matched to the capabilities of Flash. Using silhouettes instead of full-color graphics keeps the movement fast and download times low, while adding to the distinctive style.

4
Understatement is also key to the game's interface. Apart from the main screen there is just a large level countdown, a progress gauge and a display to tell the player which button to hit and when.

5
This screen reinforces the product message and pushes the user on to other related promotional activities. Note the option to send a link on to a friend—these games need word of mouth to spread.

SMIRNOFF

Better luck next time!

You've been listening to tracks mixed by Tall Paul, Brandon Block, John Kelly and Fergie.

Buy ANY 4 SMIRNOFF® Drinks at your nearest Switched On bar and collect these 4 FREE CDs.

free dance CD's!

Then have a chance to win more prizes including:
- Global clubbing trips
- VIP clubbing nights
- Sony MP3 players
- Boxfresh gear

Find nearest Switched On outlet

Why not change your luck and **enter the Switched On Dance prize draw to win groovy prizes** including **Glastonbury tickets**, a **VIP clubbing night** for you and your mates or signed copies of the Switched On dance CDs.

Enter prize draw   Play again   Challenge a friend

7

level

.02

brandon block

TELETEXT HOLIDAYS

The two pop-ups are part of a larger campaign that includes DHTML and skyscrapers. The pop ups however show the creative process very clearly. The central idea—the boredom of the dull, average day can be relieved by vivid memories of a great holiday—is a particularly strong one. Both pop-ups also transform abstract vector graphics into bitmapped holiday snaps, as if to say that a holiday has a stronger reality than normal. In addition, the color scheme of the ads matches up to the brand colors of the Teletext service.

174

I

2

5

6

7

1 | 2

The pop-up opens with this vector image of a brightly colored mug sitting on a grey office desk, artfully suggested by details such as the clock and the mouse.

3 | 4

As the image zooms in on the mug, the vector image morphs into this holiday snap bitmap as the tagline fades in. An object lesson in getting a point across succinctly.

8   **9**

5 | 6 | 7

In this second ad the shirt on the washing line provides the reminder of a perfect holiday, its bold colors standing out against the unexciting background.

8 | 9

As the image zooms in, the flat colors turn into this inviting beach vista. Again, the idea of holiday as an escape from the mundane is put in concise terms.

VIRGIN STUDENT

This Virgin website has been designed from the ground up to appeal to the needs and interests of the UK's student population. The content changes on a fairly regular basis to reflect the events of the student calendar. In the examples shown here, the site was celebrating the run up to Valentine's Day. Everything, from text to design to the interactive features, is closely targeted at a particular audience, and while there's little overt marketing, it still works to promote Virgin services in the travel, communications, and entertainment fields.

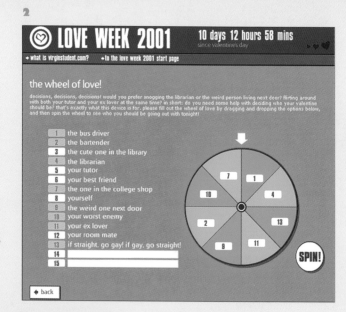

1
Virgin's site is heavily interactive, with plenty of fun content to keep its target audience entertained. The irreverent tone crosses across every aspect of the design.

2 | 3
The "wheel of love" is a case in point, jokily pointing the user at possible objects of affection. Once the wheel has spoken, the page offers options to send the word on.

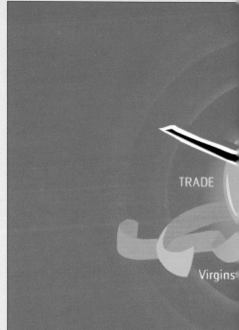

3

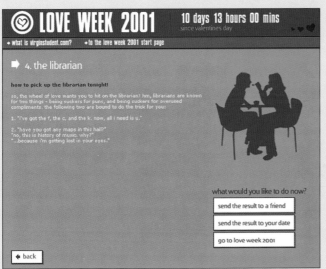

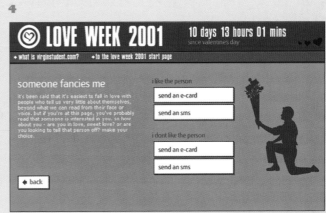

4
E-cards and SMS messages serve a dual purpose; allowing users to share the fun with friends, but also spreading information on the site to new potential users.

5
This game reinforces the proposition that Virgin holidays put together great vacations on a tight budget. If they spend less they get more—a potent message for students.

6 | 7
The player uses a sandal to rid their fIlthy hotel room of pests. The humor is perfectly pitched at student level.

6

7

URBAN KISS

This microsite for a British radio station's annual music compilation uses the classic game Frogger as a template for an urban themed update. The intention is to drive traffic to the site and collect information from the final page. To this end, users are asked to enter their details onto a leaderboard, in the hope of winning one of several prizes that are up for grabs.

2

Urban Fugative

The top scorer on our leaderboard by midday on Tuesday July 02 will win a limited edition copy of the new Ludacris video in its promo packaging, an EXCLUSIVE Musiq 12", a copy of Urban Kiss 2 PLUS albums from Ja Rule, Christina Milian, Luck & Neat and Mary J Blige. The next highest score will win a copy of Urban Kiss 2 and the goody bag of albums from Ja Rule, Christina Milian, Luck & Neat and Mary J Blige. 23 other lucky runners up will all get a copy of Urban Kiss 2.........so get 'scorin!

Home

Next

Ja Rule, Christina Milian, Luck & Neat and Mary J Blige!

Urban Fugative Game

1 | 2
The intro screen and instructions put the emphasis on the prizes to be won, including records and promotional videos from a number of well-known urban music artists. While the site also promotes the Kiss brand, it only really works if it can encourage the user to enter their details at the end. This allows the company to follow up with further promotional work through email or SMS text messages.

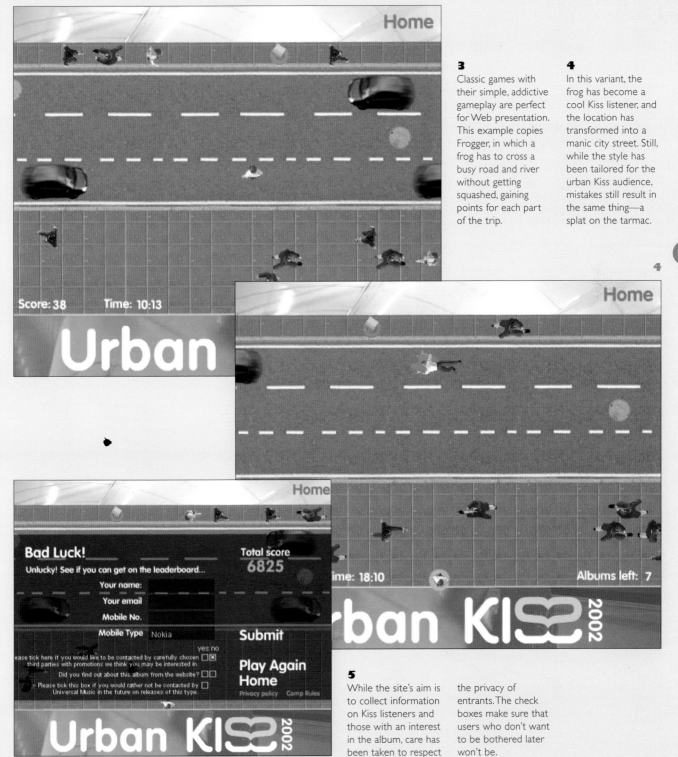

3
Classic games with their simple, addictive gameplay are perfect for Web presentation. This example copies Frogger, in which a frog has to cross a busy road and river without getting squashed, gaining points for each part of the trip.

4
In this variant, the frog has become a cool Kiss listener, and the location has transformed into a manic city street. Still, while the style has been tailored for the urban Kiss audience, mistakes still result in the same thing—a splat on the tarmac.

179

5
While the site's aim is to collect information on Kiss listeners and those with an interest in the album, care has been taken to respect the privacy of entrants. The check boxes make sure that users who don't want to be bothered later won't be.

MILKA

Here is another simple Flash game, this time for the Swiss chocolate manufacturer, Milka. The designers have chosen an appropriate Alpine theme, skiing, and turned it into a game with three different stages to race through. The graphics are necessarily kept to a very basic level, but as long as the game moves quickly and the controls are responsive this doesn't matter. Users are prepared to make many allowances when it comes to free, online games.

1
It is hard to imagine a more minimal instruction screen than this one. Those expecting a visual treat should already have a clear idea of what to expect.

2
The game provides easy, normal, and expert difficulty options in the form of a simple downhill race, a night skiing challenge and a tricky Super G competition. Milka cows provide an extra obstacle for the champion skier to contend with.

3

3 | 4

Once the race has been selected, the screen zooms in to the mountain top start where the countdown begins. Once the skiing begins the action shifts to a 3D view behind the player. Background detail has been kept low in order to maintain smooth animation, but some sense of speed is provided by the slalom poles rushing past. While Flash games are getting a lot more sophisticated, such primitive efforts will run on even the most basic computer.

4

VAUXHALL

This is a microsite that viewers are taken to from pop-ups and banners. The microsite refers to the spate of realistic driving games that have appeared on the likes of the Sony PlayStation in recent years, aping their look and feel but with one big difference: it allows users to book test drives and try out the car for real, as well as request a brochure. Users can also play a driving game in which their score is compared against those of other players. The player can choose which Vauxhall car they drive in the game, and as part of the selection process they are given information about the whole range.

182

1

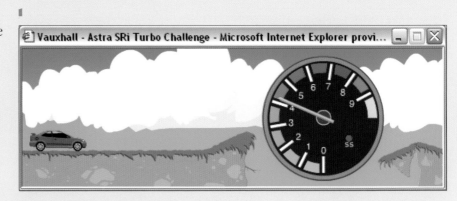

2

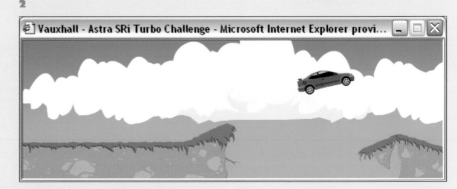

3

1 | 2 | 3
The game itself won't win any awards for innovative design, but it does work to push the message that the Astra SRi Turbo is capable of some impressive levels of performance, albeit in a rather unrealistic cartoon way.

4

This page is designed to ape the car selection screens that you would typically find in a PlayStation racing game such as Gran Turismo. While such games pride themselves on their accurate handling and immersive graphics, Vauxhall is making the point that there is nothing that can match the experience of the real thing.

5

This next screen carries on the theme. Like its in-game equivalent it has a mixture of options and specifications, but it also has links to get a brochure sent out or book a real test drive in a real car.

6

Clicking on the "Play to Win" button takes the user to the Flash screen opposite. Even the game promotes the "real is better" concept, as it offers a day of racing in a Vauxhall sports car as the main prize.

7

This mysterious pop-up lures users to the game in question. The screen is a mocked-up version of what you might see in the typical driving game. This ties in perfectly to the whole underlying concept.

5

6

7

GLOSSARY

ad banner A still or animated graphic object found on a webpage, used to advertise a product, brand or company. Banner ads are still among the most common form of advertising on the Web, and come in a variety of shapes and sizes.

ad view A single advertisement that appears in the browser display at the moment when the webpage is loaded.

animated GIF A GIF file consisting of multiple images. When displayed in a browser, the images show one after another in quick succession to simulate animation.

 186

applet A small application that performs a specific task, usually as part of a larger application. The term is also used to describe small Java programs that are downloaded by an Internet browser to perform particular functions.

authoring This is a generic term used to describe the process by which multimedia, or interactive Web environments, are created. Authoring programs are pieces of software that allow producers to put together a variety of assets in one information product. Most Web-authoring programs are in reality page layout or website construction packages.

bandwidth The rate of data crossing a communications line or system. In the case of Internet connections, this is expressed in terms of kilobits per second (Kbps), and has a direct relation to how quick the connection is between the computer browsing the Web and the server that provides the information. Most home computers connect via a modem and the public telephone system. This is the slowest form of connection and a lot of users now prefer to use the faster service provided by cable or DSL connections.

banner A graphic image, acting as an advertisement, that typically runs across the top of a webpage or sits in a designated ad-space. Banners usually conform to particular physical dimensions, file sizes and file formats.

bit The smallest unit of digital date, either a binary 0 or 1. Eight bits make up a byte, 1,024 bytes equals one kilobyte (KB), 1,024Kb equals one megabyte (MB).

brand advertising A form of advertising that is designed to create a favorable image of a brand and its full range of products and services, rather than a particular product.

browser An application that downloads content from a server on the World Wide Web, then interprets and displays it to the user in the form of webpages. The most widely used browsers are Microsoft's Internet Explorer and Netscape's Navigator. There are differences between the way that browsers display webpages.

button A clickable graphic, commonly used to load a new page or execute some other instruction. In some cases, buttons can be used as adverts.

cache A store of data held in a computer's memory or on the hard disk, used to hold and control the flow of data, including Web content, and speed up its delivery to the user.

click Any user interaction with an online advertisement that might lead to the user visiting the advertiser's destination.

click rate The percentage of ad views that result in click-throughs. This is a measure of how many viewers go on to visit the advertiser's website, and as such it is a good indication both of the effectiveness of the ad and of its placing on a site.

click-through A click where the user actually visits and sees the advertiser's website.

co-branding In online advertising, where two websites or sections within a website combine some function or feature as a joint enterprise. This might be as simple as the display of both logos, or it can be a more complex cross-venture.

cookie A small text file on the user's hard disk that identifies the user's browser to visited websites. There are two types of cookie: persistent cookies remain until they expire or are actively deleted, session cookies are erased as soon as the browser is shut down.

compression The process of reducing a file to a smaller size. A common reason for compressing a file size is to make it quicker to download from the Web.

CPM abbr.: Cost-per-thousand. The most common buying model in Web-based advertising, CPM defines the cost of 1000 impressions. Derived from print advertising, the M denotes the Roman numeral for thousand.

cross-platform The term applied to software or websites that may be run or viewed on different computer systems. Web designers should concentrate on making sure that their applications are compatible with both Macintosh- and Windows-based systems, as these two platforms are used by the majority of the world's Web audience.

DHTML abbr.: Dynamic Hypertext Markup Language. A development of basic HTML code that extends the range of possible effects to basic animations and highlighted buttons, without the need for any "plug-ins."

domain name The name, unique to each Internet site, that identifies it at a global level. Domain names are usually organized by geographic or generic designators, such as ".com," ".GOV," ".co.uk", or".org."

e-commerce Business transactions conducted across the Web. This area of Web design is very specialized and requires in-depth understanding of secure protocols and financial transactions technology.

embedding This is a technique whereby external files, usually video, animation, or sound files, are incorporated into a webpage. If the browser supports the files natively, then the embedding process is merely a way of including a reference to the file in the HTML code. If, on the other hand, there is no native support, then the embedding process can also include notifying the viewer that a specialist plug-in is required to play or view the file.

expandable banner A banner ad that expands to a larger size when a user clicks on it or moves their cursor over it.

file format The particular method used to store the digital data that makes up a computer file. Some file formats, like TIFF, JPEG, and WAV can be read by many different programs, while others, such as the Photoshop format PSD, are designed for use with a single piece of software.

Flash A vector-based file format (.swf), commonly used in interactive or animated content on the Web. Flash is developed by Macromedia, who also produce the authoring application of the same name. A flash file requires a browser plug-in to be installed in order to display its content. The advantage of Flash is that it generates small files that are correspondingly quick to download and, being vector, are scalable to any dimension without an increase in file size.

GIF abbr.: Graphic Interchange Format. A basic graphic format. GIF files are heavily compressed, which makes them quick to download, and can have transparent backgrounds. The downside is that the color palette is limited to only 256 individual colors.

hit A message sent to a website's server when a user's browser accesses a page or some element on it. Although a good measure of a server's workload, hits provide little useful information for advertisers.

homepage The page that typically provides the main point of entry into a website, providing basic navigation to other areas, and delivering a vital first impression of the content, design, and values contained within.

host A computer on any form of network (including the Internet) that provides services or information to other computers on the same network.

HTML abbr.: Hypertext Markup Language. The text-based 'page description language' that provides the basic building blocks behind the World Wide Web. The HTML code defines the contents and position of text and image elements on the page, and the user's browser interprets that code and downloads any required files in order to display them.

hyperlink An embedded link between text, pictures, buttons in a webpage, and other parts of the site or another website. Sometimes called a "hot link."

image map An image on a webpage that contains multiple links or "hotspots" that lead to different destination pages.

impression The measurement of responses from a Web server to requests from a user's browser, at the point at which that user should be able to see the page and any advertising on it. One of the basic units of Web advertising.

Internet The global system of interconnected networks that provides the backbone for email and the World Wide Web.

interstitial A commercial advertisement that appears between two webpages on a website, taking over the entire browser window before forwarding the user to their original destination. This forwarding must take place within five seconds.

intranet A network which, while using many of the same protocols and standards as the World Wide Web, is limited in accessibility to members of a particular group or organization, and used to share information or resources.

Java A programming language devised by Sun Microsystems for creating small applications that can be downloaded from a Web server and used to provide particular functions or dynamic effects.

JPEG abbr.: Joint Photographic Experts Group. An International Standards group, which defines compression standards for bitmapped color, images. The abbreviated form, pronounced "jay-peg" usually refers to the popular compressed file format. JPEG is a lossy file format, meaning that some degree of visual information is inevitably lost during compression.

microsite A small site, normally existing within a larger website, which is dedicated to a particular theme. In Web advertising, microsites are usually designed to advertise a particular product or product range, and essentially work as large-scale, multi-page adverts. Microsites are usually constructed to show rich-media content.

mouseover Where a user on a website places their mouse cursor over a button or object without clicking. On some sites, this may initiate an action, such as a small change of image or another special effect.

MP3 An audio file format used to compress digital audio files by as much as 100:1. Most often used by music sites to give visitors the best possible sound while still taking into account the restrictions of Web delivery.

MPEG acronym: Motion Picture Experts Group. An International Standards Organization that defines standards for digital video compression. MPEG1 (.mpg) is a common medium-quality video file format. MPEG2 is the high-quality format used by digital TV and DVD.

navigation system The system by which users navigate from one page of a website to another. It usually takes the form of a series of buttons.

page An online document with a specific URL, which may comprise of multiple text and graphic elements. When loaded into a Web browser, it will be recognizable as a single entity.

palette This term refers to a subset of colors that are needed to display a particular image. For instance, a GIF image will have a palette containing a maximum of 256 individual and distinct colors.

pay-per-click An online advertising model, where the advertiser pays a specific amount to the website where the ad is placed for each click-through to the advertiser's website.

PDF abbr.: Portable Document Format. A file format used in the creation of electronic documents that need to be viewed by anyone, regardless of what operating system or applications they are using. PDF was designed by Adobe, who also produce a free viewer (Acrobat Reader) which enables PDF documents to be read, and an authoring tool (Acrobat Distiller) which is used to create PDFs or convert them from other applications.

pixel abbr.: Picture Element. A single illuminated dot on a computer screen, and the usual measure of dimensions with regard to digital images, including adverts.

plug-in A small program or applet, which is installed and used as part of another

GLOSSARY

application. On the Web, plug-ins are used to add functionality to browsers, such as support for Flash files.

pop-under A Web advert that appears in a separate window beneath the browser window, where it is hidden until the user closes, moves, or resizes that window.

pop-up A Web advert that appears in a separate window on top of the browser window, usually disappearing after a limited period. A pop-up may contain text, graphics, links, or animation.

rich media Any online content beyond basic text and still images, including sound, music, video, animation or interactive elements. Rich media typically incorporates technologies such as streaming video, Flash, JavaScript, and DHTML.

rollover button A graphic button type that changes in appearance when the mouse pointer moves over it.

search engine A webpage or Web-based applet that helps Web users to find information or websites on the Internet. In most cases, a complex database of terms, links and other resources is queried through the use of keywords entered by the user.

SGML abbr.: Standard Generalized Markup Language. A basic page description language used to define documents that can be read on any computer. The parent of HTML, XML, and WML.

shockwave A file format developed by Macromedia, the company behind Flash. Shockwave files require a Shockwave browser plug-in, and while the format includes support for animation, video, and audio, it specializes in rich interactive content, including 3D graphics.

skyscraper A common format for Web-based advertising; a tall, thin box that usually appears at the side of a webpage.

SMS abbr.: Short Message Service. A short text file sent to a mobile, SMS-enabled device (usually a mobile phone).

spam Unwanted and unsolicited email.

stickiness A measure of how good a website is at holding on to visitors. The longer the duration of the average visit, the more "sticky" the content must be.

superstitial Unicast's interstitial ad format. A superstitial is cached by the browser before playback, and must be of set dimensions (550 × 480), length (20 second) and file size (100Kb).

surfing Term used to describe the act of searching for material on the World Wide Web.

targeting The practice of purchasing advertising space on particular websites with the aim of reaching a specific audience for a specific campaign.

third-party ad server A server maintained by an independent company, who handles the business of managing and tracking a Web-based advertising campaign for a number of clients. Such companies specialize in targeted campaigns.

traffic Term used to describe the number of visitors a specific website receives.

transitional An ad displayed between webpages, in the same manner as an interstitial.

URL abbr.: Uniform Resource Locator. The unique address of a webpage on the Web, consisting of a resource type (www), a domain name (company.com), and a page locater (home.htm)

viral marketing An Internet ad campaign, the success of which relies on individuals sending material associated with the product, either a game, animation or video, to a number of friends, who in turn send it on to more friends.

WAP acronym: Wireless Application Protocol. The system of communications protocols used by wireless devices—particularly mobile phones—to access the Internet.

websafe Color that will not be changed when an image is optimized for the Web.

website A series of webpages linked together to form a coherent presence on the Web.

XML abbr.: eXtensible Markup Language. A successor to HTML, which uses HTML-style tags to describe richer or more dynamic content. Currently used to transfer complex data or create applications on the Web.

INDEX

189

Showcase URLs

Ali G (pages 136–137)
www.alig.com

Angel/Buffy (pages 138–139)
www.buffy.com

Audi (pages 140–141)
www.almapbbdo.com.br/cannes/audi/halfacar/page.html
www.audi.com

Bacardi Breezer (pages 142–143)
www.bacardibreezer.co.uk

BetInternet (pages 144–145)
www.betinterbet.com

BMW (pages146–151)
www.bmw.com

BT Open World (pages 152–153)
www.btopenworld.com

Cult Films/Nintendo Game Cube (pages 154–155)
www.nintendogamecube.com

The Green Party (pages 156–157)
www.ae–pro.com/thegarden

Brilliant Industries
(pages 158–159)
www.new.egg.com

iVillage (pages 160–161)
www.ivillage.co.uk

Land Rover (pages 162–163)
www.landrover.com
www.autoexpress.co.uk

Nike football (pages 164–165)
www.nikefootball.nike.com

Puma (pages 166–167)
www.shudoh.com

Scooby Doo (pages 168–169)
www.scoobydoo.com

Shoks (pages 170–171)
www.hulahoops.co.uk/eelextrix

Smirnoff (pages 172–173)
www.smirnoff.com

Teletext Holidays (pages 174–175)
www.teletextholidays.co.uk

Virgin Student (pages 176–177)
www.virginstudent.com

Urban Kiss (pages 178–179)
www.kiss100.com

Milka (pages 180–181)
www.milkaski.com

Vauxhall (pages 182–183)
www.vauxhall.co.uk

Copyright Notice